SOMEWHERE IN PERSIA

SOMEWHERE IN PERSIA

MEMOIRS OF A WAR CORRESPONDENT

DWARD LEE GREENBIRD

SURREAL PRIMITIVE

all my best
Dward Lee Greenbird

Contents

SOMEWHERE IN PERSIA

Introduction

THIS BOOK is a collection of photographs and writings, both published and personal that my father, Corporal Sam Greenberg, created while he was a war correspondent in the Army, based in Iran during World War II. He was stationed with the M. T. S. or Motor Transport Service that was involved with logistics; they sent "lend-lease" supplies, provided by the United States, from Iran to Russia.

Their headquarters were based in Bandar Shapur, a port city on the Persian Gulf, where my father spent most of his time. During World War II, Bandar Shapur consisted of a jetty, two shipping berths, a railhead, and some warehouses, with the closest civilian settlement being some miles distant. He traveled over much of Iran and also visited Iraq and Jerusalem during his leave time before finishing his military service.

Sam Greenberg was born in 1912, in Philadelphia, PA. He was almost always seen with a smile on his face and was a pretty happy guy. He loved baseball. I remember him teaching me to ice skate when I was three; his skates were hockey skates, so I'm guessing he played. One of three children born to Anna and Herman Greenberg, he attended school in Philadelphia.

Chapter One

MY FATHER'S ALBUMS AND SCRAPBOOK

MOST OF THE PHOTOS used in this book came from two albums of Sam's pictures. He bought the first album here in the States. The second album he bought in Jerusalem.

The first photo album is primarily of equipment from the U.S. Army before World War II. You can see an airship embossed on the cover of the first photo album.

During the years between 1908 and 1937 the U.S. Army had a program to operate airships.[1]

First Photo Album

Next is a photo of the album that Sam bought in Jerusalem. It is made of embossed leather with a pressed low-relief plate made of copper depicting David's Tower which is located in Jerusalem.

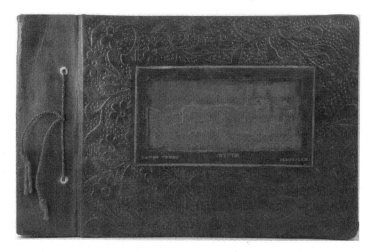

Second Photo Album

All of the articles that I used for this book came from the scrapbook my father started when he graduated from high school in 1930 and added to until 1948. In the book he kept everything that he'd had published and some personal unpublished essays, as well as letters to home, and articles he found interesting.

After graduating high school, Dad went to Temple University but quit after only six months. By then he knew for certain what he wanted to do and dropped out of Temple to work at a Philadelphia newspaper called the Public Ledger. The Public Ledger was the first of three different newspapers he would work for in his writing career. The next newspaper was the Miami Tribune in Miami, Florida.

He enlisted in April of 1942 and became a war correspondent for the U. S. Army in September of that year. Sam wrote for the military until

March 1945 and ended his service the following October. After the war, he worked for the newspaper once again, this time in Columbus, Georgia. The morning edition was the Columbus Enquirer and the afternoon edition was known as the Columbus Ledger.

The following are some full-page images from the scrapbook. Unfortunately, the original pages are yellowed from age due to the inferior quality of the paper that was used, not just in the scrapbook itself, but the newsprint paper and other publications. To edit images and reproduce the scrapbook for Somewhere in Persia, I used a MacBook Pro laptop with the Mojave operating system. Adobe Illustrator CC 2018 was indispensable, as well as Affinity Photo, ver. 1.6.6. The scanner I used was an EPSON Perfection V37 and most images were replicated at 300 dpi. Files were created primarily in .jpg format.

Here is one full page from the Scrapbook.

Here is another full page from the Scrapbook.

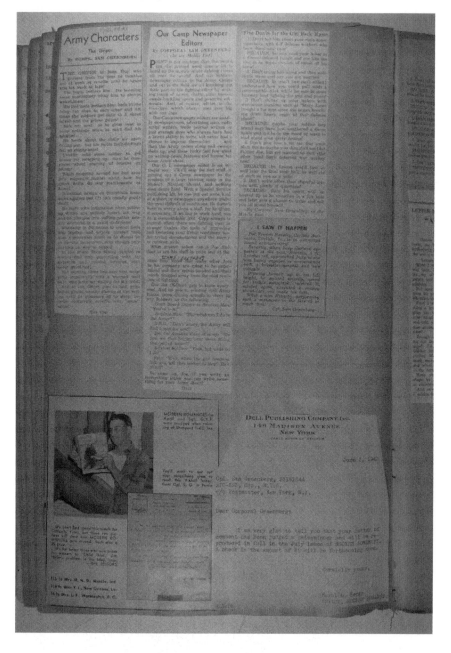

In most of the photos, Sam wrote descriptions in their white borders. I have typed up that information for clarity. Some of those borders contain names of cities and areas which were accurate in his day, but have since had the spellings altered. Throughout the book, I chose to use the spellings Sam used.

In a few cases, it was necessary that I enhance the images by brightening them or removing unintentional marks, but for the most part the image files presented in this book are as close to exact replication as possible. Mostly I wanted to get rid of the yellowed paper and make the entries more readable.

———————

A note on endnotes at the back of the book

In some cases, the wording of some endnotes has been slightly changed to fit the style of the book. Every effort has been made to get complete information and permissions, however that was not possible for every endnote. All sources given were checked to be accurate as of the date of this printing.

Chapter Two

FAMILY

As to the letters Sam sent home to family, most were addressed to Mom, Pop, Gilda, and Herman. Mom and Pop were Anna and William Greenberg. Gilda was Sam's sister and Herman, his brother. William and Anna Greenberg emigrated from Russia to the United States in 1903.

The next photo was taken in the Germantown section of Philadelphia, Pennsylvania in June of 1949. In the photo, Pop is on the left in the white shirt. Sam's mom, Anna sits next to William on his left. To Anna's  left, leaning in, is Gilda. The mother with child is Ruth Greenberg, Sam's wife and my mother. She is holding my brother, Arthur. I was not born until the following year, September 1950.

My mother's parents died when she was 12 and 14. The only grandparent that I met was Anna Greenberg.

The next photo is an early
view of my family, the
Greenbergs, taken in January of 1953. Sam is holding
me. My mother is holding
my sister, Gale and to her
left is my brother, Arthur.

I hope you enjoy reading my father's writing and about his experiences
and observations during World War II. Through this book, I hope you
will get to know Sam Greenberg a bit. He wanted the world to see
and hear his story.

Chapter Three

BEFORE THE WAR

SAM MOVED TO MIAMI in 1934, and worked at the Miami Tribune from 1934 until his military service with the U.S. Army began in 1942. Here are two articles Sam found of interest while working at the Miami Tribune.

The first article was titled "Anti-Semitism Here" and was published in December, 1938.

The article talks of antisemitism in the United States in the late 1930's and earlier in the 1920's, including stating that "this latest wave of Jew haters will not rise very high." When addressing the subject of Gentiles and Jews marrying, Sam states that the best thing this country can do is go on being the melting pot of the many diversities that we find in the United States.

If you have trouble reading the scan of the newspaper article, the following is a copy of the text.

ANTI-SEMITISM HERE

Congress shall make no law respecting an establishment of religion, or prohibiting the free exercise thereof; or abridging the freedom of speech or of the press; or the right of the people peaceably to assemble and to petition the Government for a redress of grievances.

—Amendment 1, United States Constitution.

The above is the first of the ten items in the American Bill of Rights, adopted 147 years ago yesterday.

Jew Haters Increasing

The first part of it means that our Government shall not officially discriminate against any religion. It does not mean that Americans are forbidden to dislike other Americans on religious or any other grounds.

Plenty of people just now are exercising their right to dislike the Jews. Major Gen. George V. H. Moseley (retired), for example, says, in what at least sounds like an anti-Semitic utterance:

Who ... remembers our making any protest worth while when a party of less than 2% of the Russian people brought 160,000,000 Russians under the control of the most tyrannical government known to history?

As a matter of fact, we went to war with the Bolshevik Government over that revolution, and we refused to recognize that Government for sixteen years. Could any more strenuous protest have been made?

As another illustration of the anti-Semitic wave now building up here, The News yesterday printed a digest of a pamphlet gotten out by a post office-box publisher and listing a large number of Jews connected with the New Deal.

The list looked to us more like a tribute than an insult to the Jews, though, of course, it was intended as an insult and an incitement to political if not mob action against them.

★★★

The Answer: "So What?"

For example, Secretary of State Cordell Hull was listed as having "married Frances, daughter of Isaac Witz, of Staunton, Va." Mayor LaGuardia's one-quarter or one-eighth Jewish blood (nobody ever seems to know the exact fraction) was duly publicized once more. William C. Bullitt, Ambassador to France, was alleged to have had a Jewish mother.

The answer to all these charges is: So what? So Mr. Hull is a distinguished and successful Secretary of State, just as before that he was a powerful political force and sagacious Senator from Tennessee; Mayor LaGuardia is usually considered the best Mayor New York ever had, and is the only reform Mayor we ever re-elected; Mr. Bullitt is one of the ablest and best liked men in our diplomatic corps.

Gov. Lehman and Secretary Morgenthau, also named on this list, are further examples of excellent discharge of their duties.

The list also includes Robert Moses, our Jewish Park Commissioner, and the best one we've had yet. Mr. Moses, incidentally, is married to a Gentile woman, and their union is one of the happiest on any record.

★★★

Let the Melting Pot Go on Boiling

We doubt that this wave of anti-Semitism will rise very high. We've had them before—notably in the early 20's, when the Ku Klux Klan set out to put down both the Catholics and Jews, and presently folded up. Its ghost goes mumbling on, but few take it seriously.

We don't want to be understood as saluting all Jews as practically perfect people. There are worthwhile Jews and worthless Jews, just as is the case with Gentiles, Negroes, Chinese or Indians.

But we do maintain that what racial faults the Old World Jews have displayed are disappearing in the American melting pot.

The old-time charge that the Jews were slick at a trade, too slick, but not truly manly—not athletes—has now been pretty well washed up, to mention only a few, Harry Danning of the Giants, Phil Weintraub of the Phillies, Hank Greenberg of the Detroit Tigers; by Marshall Goldberg and Benny Friedman in football; by Max Baer and numerous other sluggers in the ring. Physically, the Jews average out as well as any other group.

Another longstanding complaint against the Jews has been that they would not assimilate with other races; that they held themselves a race apart, and rather better than anybody else. Well, in this country they are intermarrying more and more with Gentiles. We're glad to see that trend, and hope it continues and increases.

The best thing this country can do, we believe, is just to go on being the Melting Pot.

"The Jews Who Have Fought in America's Wars" was published in the Miami Tribune in January, 1941.

It describes people of the Jewish faith and ethnicity fighting for America from the American Revolution to World War I and how this great country was built, from its foundation up, by people of all kinds, of many different nationalities and religions.

Again, reprinted for clarity.

The Mail Bag

The Jews Who Have Fought in America's Wars

The Record is printing today a letter from Judge Joseph L. Kun, of Common Pleas Court No. 1, the anonymous letter referred to in Judge Kun's letter, and his reply to it. We feel the way Judge Kun does about anonymous letters; but we believe the subject is sufficiently interesting to warrant this space in the Mail Bag.

To the Editor:

In The Record of Wednesday, December 25, 1940, in the article with the caption "Jews Here Begin Feast of Light," you quoted something I said the night before at Temple Beth Israel, 32d st. and Montgomery ave., in connection with the synagogue's centennial celebration, part of which was, "Our forefathers fought side by side with Washington and helped sow the seeds of liberty and freedom Americans now enjoy."

This morning I received in the mail the inclosed anonymous letter signed "American." While it is against my policy to answer anonymous letters in any way, yet as the writer indicates the medium of reply as The Record and is apparently quite ignorant of the facts on the subject. I thought it would do no harm to prepare a short answer and ask you to publish it if your own policy will permit you to do so under the circumstances. Unfortunately, I do not have the address of the writer of the letter.

Joseph L. Kun, Judge
Court of Common Pleas No. 1

The Anonymous Letter

Dear Sir:

Would be very much interested in knowing of just one Jew who fought in any American war, not alone with Washington.

Will look forward to your answer in The Record, from which this clipping was taken.

(The clipping referred to, inclosed with "American's" letter, was The Record's account of Judge Kun's address at Temple Beth Israel.)

Many more Americans are waiting for the same thing.

AMERICAN.

Judge Kun's Reply

To the Editor:

"American" has asked for some information about Jews who have fought in American wars. Official Government records show the following:

Jews fought in the American Revolution under Washington from 1776 on. Some of the names are Lieutenant

Colonel Solomon Bush, Major Lewis Bush, who was killed at the Battle of Brandywine; Philip Minnis, Nathaniel Levy, Marx Lazarus, Moses Cohen, William Levy, David Judah, Colonel Isaac Franks, Benjamin Nones, who was on General Washington's staff. There were many others.

In the War of 1812, largely a naval war, there were Commodore Uriah P. Levy, the first Jew to hold high rank in the United States Navy, and Captain John Ondroneaux, a French Jew who became one of the most daring privateersmen during that war.

There was also Mordecai Myers, who distinguished himself at the battle of Sacketts Harbor; Aaron Levy, who was a lieutenant colonel in the army; Judah Touro, of New Orleans, who gave his services to Andrew Jackson in the defense of that city in 1815.

There was also the famous Seixas family, who distinguished themselves to such an extent that there was a company in the army called the Seixas Company.

In the Mexican War of 1848, Jews served at the Alamo, at Goliad and on the battlefield of San Jacinto. Some of the names are Benjamin H. Mordecai, M. K. Moses, Herman Ehrenberg, and among those who fell at the Alamo was A. Wolf. A Dr. David De Leon, an army surgeon, so distinguished himself by taking command of the forces when the commanding officer of the regiment fell, that he earned the title "fighting doctor."

10,000 Jews in War Between States.

In the great Civil War between the States, Jews flocked to the colors of the States in which they happened to live, each loyal to his own to such an extent that there were many instances, as was the case with Christians, that members of the same family fought against each other. There were about 10,000 Jews in the armed forces during the Civil War, of which about 6000 were in the Union Army and about 4000 in the Confederate army.

It is to be noted that although the Jewish population in the country at that time was less than one-half percent of the total, more than 6 percent of the Jewish population responded to the colors.

Among the Jews in both armies were nine generals, 18 colonels, eight lieutenant colonels, 40 staff officers, 200 captains, 325 lieutenants, 48 adjutants, 25 surgeons and one chaplain, the Rev. Dr. Arnold Fischel, who was the first Jewish chaplain in the United States Army.

The highest ranking Jewish officer was Major General Frederick Kneffler, a Union commander. Edward S. Salomon was a brigadier general, and Leopold Blumenberg helped to organize the 5th Maryland Regiment, of which he became major.

Gen. Salomon Later Govenor.

On the Confederate side there were equally notable Jews. At the famous battle of Gettysburg there were approximately 1000 Jews who fought on both sides, outstanding of whom was General Edward Salomon of Illinois. He was later appointed Governor of the territory of Washington by President U. S. Grant.

At the conclusion of the war, five Jewish soldiers received the Congressional Medal of Honor: Sergeant Major Abraham Cohen, Sergeant Leopold Karpelis, and three privates, Abraham Greenwald, Benjamin Levy and David Orbansky.

In the next war, the Spanish-American, which was of
short duration, more than 6000 Jews were in the service,
of whom about 100 were in the navy. In the first battle
by Teddy Roosevelt's Rough Riders, of the 15 Americans killed four were of Jewish faith. One of the second
lieutenants of the Rough Riders was Samuel Greenwald.
There was also Lieutenant Colonel Abraham Harbach,
who later became colonel.

First to Die in Philippines.

Down in the Philippines, the first American volunteer
killed in the attack on Manila was Sergeant Maurice
Justh, of the 1st California Volunteers, a regiment which
included 90 Jews.

Other Jews who did notable work in that campaign
were Dr. Joseph Heller, who won praise for his courage
in administering to wounded under fire; Solomon Goth-
man, of the 1st Colorado Volunteers; Sergeant Morris J.
Cohen, of the 20th Kansas Volunteers, who was killed
after winning fame as captor of the first flag taken from
the enemy.

On the naval side, Ernest Suntznich, a Jew, was the
first American sailor to die in the war. He was killed
during the bombardment of Cienfuegos. The only
American sailor killed during the battle of Santiago
was Edward Gratz, chief master-at-arms on the warship
Oregon. Commander Adolph Marix was second in
command on the Iowa in the battle of Santiago. Much
more could be added; space does not permit.

In the great World War, the records show that there
were about 225,000 Jews in the various branches of
the armed forces. Of these, 171,000 were in the army,

23,500 in the navy, 12,250 in the Marine Corps, and 18,000 in other branches of the service. There were 10,000 Jewish commissioned officers in the several branches of the service.

100 Colonels in World War.

In the army there were more than 100 colonels and lieutenant colonels, over 500 majors, 1500 captains and 6000 lieutenants.

In the navy there were over 900 commissioned officers, the highest rank being reached by Rear Admiral Joseph Strauss, who was in command of the mine-laying squadron in the North Sea.

In the Marine Corps there were at least 100 Jewish officers, the highest of whom was Brigadier General Charles H. Laucheimer.

About 3500 Jews died in the war; 1800 in action, 600 of wounds and 1100 through accident and other causes. There were in addition 12,000 Jews who were wounded.

The best evidence of the high quality of Jewish courage in the World War is to be found in the official citations for gallantry in action or devotion above and beyond the call of duty. No less than 1100 citations for valor were conferred on Jewish soldiers in the American army. Of these 723 were conferred by the American command, 287 by the French, 33 by the British and 46 by various other Allied commands.

Congressional Medal for Six.

The rare Congressional Medal of Honor was won by six Jews. The Distinguished Service Cross is worn by 150, the French Medaille Militaire by four American

Jews and the Croix de Guerre by 174 Jews in the A. E. F.

It is hoped that the foregoing statement of facts will tend to make "American" a more understanding one, and to appreciate the fact that this great country of ours has been built up from its very foundation through the loyalty, devotion and co-operation of people of all kinds, of all nationalities, of all religious faiths, and that all who do so have the same and equal right to call themselves American.

JOSEPH L. KUN.

Chapter Four

1942

U. S. Army at Fort George G. Mead

SAM GREENBERG ENTERED the U. S. Army for active service at Fort George G. Mead, Maryland on April 14, 1942. During World War II, Fort George G. Mead was a basic training boot camp where new military personnel were given first instructions.

During boot camp, he wrote a short personal note. Pictured here, the note reads: "Here's food for thought: 'What many of us need most is a good vigorous kick in the seat of the can'ts!"

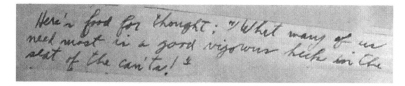

Atlanta QM Motor Base

Next, my dad was stationed at Atlanta Quartermaster Motor Base in Atlanta, Georgia.

"The Atlanta Ordnance Depot was established on February 2, 1942… the depot was conceived as a troop housing project and a Motor Repair Base."

"The Atlanta Base Shop was a fifth echelon shop where engines were rebuilt on a mass production assembly line."

"…the Command of Atlanta Base supervised the distribution of motor vehicle parts that supplied 40% of all the motor transport vehicles in the Army."[1]

Sam Greenberg received $1.00 for a fact about the Atlanta Quartermaster Motor Base that was published in "It Happened in Georgia," The Journal Sunday Magazine, The Atlanta Journal. The date was Sunday, September 27, 1942.

If you have trouble reading the scan of the newspaper article, the following is a copy of the text.

"It Happened in Georgia"

All the streets at the Atlanta Ordnance Motor Base are named for old automobiles that are no longer built—live streets commemorating dead cars.

Private Sam Greenberg, Atlanta

Here is a letter received from the office of the editor of Screen Guide dated September 29, 1942. It is in response to a letter Sam sent to the editor. His letter was chosen for reprint in the December issue of Screen Guide. He received a check for $10.00. Screen Guide was known as "Hollywood's News-Picture Magazine."

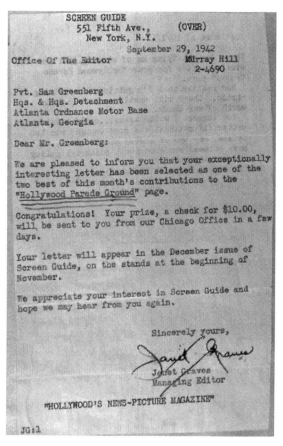

Here is a reprint of the letter for clarity.

                                    Screen Guide
                          551 Fifth Ave.,(OVER)
                                 New York, N.Y.
                            September 29, 1942
                   Office Of The Editor Mirray Hill
                                      2-4690

Pvt. Sam Greenberg
Hqs. & Hqs. Detachment
Atlanta Ordnance Motor Base
Atlanta, Georgia

Dear Mr. Greenberg:

We are pleased to inform you that your exception-
ally interesting letter has been selected as one
of the two best of this month's contributions to
the "Hollywood Parade Ground" page.
Congratulations! Your prize, a check for $10.00
will be sent to you from our Chicago Office in
a few days.
Your letter will appear in the December issue of
Screen Guide, on the stands at the beginning of
November.
We appreciate your interest in Screen Guide and
hope we may hear from you again.

                                  Sincerely yours,
                                  Janet Graves
                                  Managing Editor

        "HOLLYWOOD'S NEWS-PICTURE MAGAZINE"

JG:1

The following is a scanned copy of the article about the letter Sam
sent to Screen Guide. It was published in the December 1942 edition.

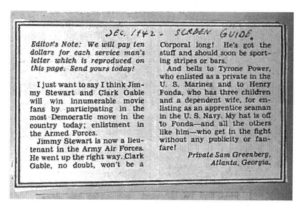

For ease of reading, here is a copy of the article.

*Editor's Note: We will pay ten dollars for each service man's
letter which is reproduced on this page. Send yours today!*

I just want to say I think Jimmy Stewart and Clark
Gable will win innumerable movie fans by participat-
ing in the most Democratic move in the country today;
enlistment in the Armed Forces.

Jimmy Stewart is now a lieutenant in the Army Air
Forces. He went up the right way. Clark Gable, no doubt,
won't be a Corporal long! He's got the stuff and should
soon be sporting stripes and bars.

And bells to Tyrone Power, who enlisted as a private
in the U. S. Marines and to Henry Fonda, who has
three children and a dependent wife, for enlisting as an
apprentice seaman in the U. S. Navy. My hat is off to
Fonda—and all the others like him—who get in the
fight without any publicity or fanfare!

Private Sam Greenberg,
Atlanta, Georgia

Somewhere downtown, we find Sam while stationed at the Atlanta
Quartermaster Motor Base.

This poem was printed in an army publication. He writes of how one
can make seemingly small steps in making money and how these steps
will add up to a much larger amount.

POETRIX

—PRIZEWINNER—

NOW, Make Small Contests Count,
THEN, Watch Dollars Mount!
    Atlanta Ordnance Motor Base,
    Pvt. Sam Greenberg,
    Georgia.

Another of many articles that Sam wrote for army publications, this one was printed in a section called: "Army Characters." He is talking about the new soldier that is far from perfect. He describes how he gets through a day. It is titled: "Boys, Meet the Messer-Upper."

For ease of reading, here is a copy of the article.

ARMY CHARACTERS

Boys, Meet the Messer-Upper
By Pvt. Sam Greenberg

Hqs. & Hqs. Detachment, Ordnance
Motor Base, Atlanta, Georgia

The ,Messer-Upper, in a sense, is not a Griper ★ ★ ★ he's a Groper! He gropes through each day as though he had just finished his first ride in an airplane pilot cabin trainer (or like a soldier, home on his first furlough, on a crowded city street among civilians only!).

In the morning he usually climbs out of wrong side of bed and has to reach way under bed to grab for his G. I. shoes. No socks are placed neatly inside each shoe, so he soon

ARMY CHARACTERS

Boys, Meet the Messer-Upper

By Pvt. Sam Greenberg,
Hqs. & Hqs. Detachment, Ordnance
Motor Base, Atlanta, Georgia.

The ,Messer-Upper, in a sense, is not a Griper . . . he's a Groper! He gropes through each day as though he had just finished his first ride in an airplane pilot cabin trainer (or like a soldier, home on his first furlough, on a crowded city street among civilians only!).

In the morning he usually climbs out of wrong side of bed and has to reach way under bed to grab for his G. I. shoes. No socks are placed neatly inside each shoe, so he soon starts a hasty haphazard search through foot locker for a clean pair of socks. After some ruffled rummaging he winds up with the socks and manages to get dressed without any further mishaps!

He encounters no trouble in sweeping and mopping up about his bunk area as both these implements of cleanliness have been brought in by other soldiers who, fortunately, are not obsessed with Gropitis.

In shaving he encounters the difficult task of rounding up all his accessories. Brushing his teeth adds up to another momentous problem. But Gropers always persevere. Some persistent searching and our Groper is soon in the latrine before a mirror. The actual mechanics of shaving never stump him. He takes this matutinal task in stride!

You can bet most all the time that he'll fall out without overseas cap or fatigue hat. Where'd I put it last night, he'll mumble.

During daily calisthenic drills, he's bound to mess up by being singled out as one whose under shirt is a bit crummy. To himself he'll alibi, where did I put that clean shirt last night.

Sugar, salt, pepper, mustard and jam are in containers. If carelessly, contents can be spilled over mess hall table. You can count on our messer-upper to single out one container and commit minor mayhem while in the process of handling same.

Out on the drill field watch his rifle, especially on "to the rear march," "to the right flank" and "to the left flank" commands. He really gropes out there, so watch your "conk."

Leave it to our Messer-Upper at mail call to horn in often and shout "Here," have a piece of mail tossed his way, look over the envelope and then toss same back, interrupting mail call by shouting "This ain't for me!"

He's the guy who dishes out daffy dilly-dailies at a dance, usually spouting spifties that prove embarrassing to a soldier and his gal, or vice versa.

In conclusion, the Messer-Upper is a guy who "gropes grearily grough the gray!"

starts a hasty haphazard search through foot locker for a clean pair of socks. After some ruffled rummaging he winds up with the socks and manages to get dressed without any further mishaps!

He encounters no trouble in sweeping and mopping up about his bunk area as both these implements of cleanliness have been brought in by other soldiers who, fortunately, are not obsessed with Gropitis.

In shaving he encounters the difficult task of rounding up all his accessories. Brushing his teeth adds up to another momentous problem. But Gropers always persevere. Some persistent searching and our Groper is soon in the latrine before a mirror. The actual mechanics of shaving never stump him. He takes this matutinal task in stride!

You can bet most all the time that he'll fall out without overseas cap or fatigue hat. Where'd I put it last night, he'll mumble.

During daily calisthenic drills, he's bound to mess up by being singled out as one whose under shirt is a bit crummy. To himself he'll alibi, where did I put that clean shirt last night.

Sugar, salt, pepper, mustard and jam are in containers. If carelessly, contents can be spilled over mess hall table. You can count on our messer-upper to single out one container and commit minor mayhem while in the process of handling same.

Out on the drill field watch his rifle, especially on "to the rear march," "to the right flank" and "to the left flank" commands. He really gropes out there, so watch your "conk."

Leave it to our Messer-Upper at mail call to horn

in often and shout "Here," have a piece of mail tossed his way, look over the envelope and then toss same back, interrupting mail call by shouting "This ain't for me!"

He's the guy who dishes out daffy dilly-dallies at a dance, usually spouting spifties that prove embarrassing to a soldier and his gal, or vice versa.

In conclusion, the Messer-Upper is a guy who "gropes grearily grough the gray!"

Carlisle Barracks

Sam saw actress Judy Garland on October 3, 1942, at Carlisle Barracks in Carlisle, Pennsylvania. He wrote a short article about her giving an autograph.

I SAW IT HAPPEN

Pvt. Francis Haverty, Carlisle Barracks, Carlisle, Pa., is an autograph hound extraordinary!

Recently, when Judy Garland appeared at the post, Haverty, 5 ft., 3 inches tall, approached Judy as she was busily engaged in conversation with a brigadier-general and two colonels.

Drawing himself up to his full height, he saluted smartly, asked for Judy's autograph, received it, saluted again, executed a snappy about-face and made his exit.

What a man Haverty—performing such a maneuver in the face of so much rank!

Cpl. Sam Greenberg

Judy Garland in Presenting "Lily Mars." 1943 [2]

"Judy Garland...was an American singer, actress, dancer, and vaudevillian. She made more than two dozen films with MGM. Garland was released from MGM in 1950, after 15 years with the studio. Her film appearances diminished, but she went on to make record-breaking concert appearances, released eight studio albums, and hosted her own Emmy-nominated television series, The Judy Garland Show. At age 39, Garland became the youngest and first female recipient of the Cecil B. DeMille Award for lifetime achievement in the film industry.[3]

"In 1938, she was cast in her most memorable role, as the young Dorothy Gale in The Wizard of Oz (1939)..."[4]

When I was a child in the 1950s, they showed The Wizard of Oz every year. I remember her singing the song "Over the Rainbow."

Camp Lee

Sam was stationed at Camp Lee starting on October 15, 1942, through early February 1943. Camp Lee was located in Prince George's County, Virginia. Camp Lee was the Quartermaster Replacement Training Center. The Quartermaster Corps is a branch of the United States Army. It is one of three U.S. Army logistics branches whose mission is to sustain general supply during peace and war.

Chapter Five

1943

BEFORE LEAVING CAMP LEE for his assignment overseas, Sam wrote the following article which was published in Photoplay Magazine.

> Both film fan magazines, Photoplay Magazine merged with Movie Mirror Magazine in 1941.[1]

The article was about draft dodgers, movie stars, and civilians and was published in the February 1943 edition. Sam received $1.00 for the article. His handwritten copy is in the scrapbook above the printed article.

PHOTOPLAY - MOVIE MIRROR
FEB. 1943

$1.00 PRIZE
Corporal to the Defense

YOUR inside story of the status of male movie stars not drafted by the Army as yet should answer once and for all the "beefing" (?) by the public about male movie-star draft dodgers!

Just because a famous movie male is single and not in the Army at present is no reason why there should be a wave of vicious talk by the public and fans that said person is a draft dodger!

Suppose the film star were just an average civilian. Then no stigma would be attached to him because he is a nonentity—an average civilian. There are thousands of civilians (unknown) who should be in the Army and are not ... but no word of reproach is attached to them because they are not famous.

Let's not ever condemn any man, movie star or John Doe, about being a draft dodger without first weighing all facts. Besides, whose business is it but the Selective Service Draft Boards (or Washington)!

Cpl. Sam Greenberg,
Camp Lee, Va.

Motor Transport Service Headquarters Persian Gulf Service Command

As a new soldier stationed at Camp Amirabad in the Persian Gulf Service Command, the first thing Sam wrote was an essay titled, "On Being Grateful." He thanked his mother, father, brother, friends, working acquaintances, and other individuals for their help and guidance in living one's life. He begins by expressing his gratitude for the time that being a soldier during the war gives him, so he can use the medium of writing to help build up morale.

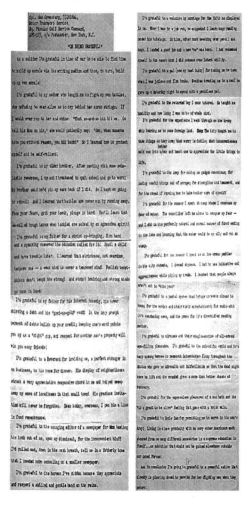

The following is a copy of Sam's unpublished text.

Cpl. Sam Greenberg, 33181644,
Motor Transport Service,
Hq. Persian Gulf Service Command,
APO–523, c/o Postmaster, New York, N.Y.

⋆ON BEING GRATEFUL⋆

As a soldier I'm grateful in time of war to be able to find time to build up morale via the writing medium and thus, in turn, build up my own morale!

I'm grateful to my mother who taught me to fight my own battles, she refusing to ever allow me to cry behind her apron strings. If I would ever run to her and whine: "That so-and-so kid hit me. Go tell his Mom on him," she would patiently say: "Son, when someone hits you without reason, you hit back!" So I learned how to protect myself and be self-reliant!

I'm grateful to my older brother. After meeting with some scholastic reverses, I up and threatened to quit school and go to work! My brother said he'd pin my ears back if I did. So I kept on going to school! And I learned that battles are never won by running away. Face your fears, grit your teeth, plunge in hard! You'll learn that so-called tough tasks when tackled are solved by an aggressive spirit!

I'm grateful to my father for a strict up-bringing, firm hand and a spanking whenever the occasion called for it! Spoil a child and have trouble later. I learned that strictness, not overdone, tempers one—a weak mind is never a tempered mind! Foolish temptations don't tempt the strong! And strict training and strong minds go hand in hand!

I'm grateful to my father for his inherent honesty, his never shirking a debt and his "good-as-gold" word! In the Army prompt payment of debts builds up your credit; keeping one's word points you up as a "right" guy, and respect for another man's property will win you many friends!

I'm grateful to a Revered for inviting me, a perfect stranger in on business, to his home for dinner. His display of neighborliness struck a very appreciative responsive chord in me and helped sweep away my wave of loneliness in that small town! His gracious invitation will never be forgotten. Even today, overseas, I pen him a line in fond remembrance!

I'm grateful to the managing editor of a newspaper for bawling the heck out of me, upon my dismissal, for the inconvenient bluff I'd pulled and, in the next breath, tell me in a fatherly tone that I needed more schooling on a smaller newspaper.

I'm grateful to the horses I've ridden because they appreciate and respect a skilled and gentle hand on the reins.

I'm grateful to a relative by marriage for the faith he displayed in me. When I was in a job rut, he suggested I learn copy reading under his tutelage. In time, after much sweating over pencil and copy, I landed a good job and a new "me" was born. I had redeemed myself in the sense that I did possess some latent ability.

I'm grateful to a pal (now my best buddy) for taking me to town when I was jobless and flat broke. Besides treating me to a meal he gave up a Saturday night to spend with a penniless pal.

I'm grateful to a retarded boy I once tutored. He taught me humility and how lucky I was to be of whole mind.

I'm grateful for the experience I went through on the troop ship bearing me to some foreign land. The trip taught me to take things as they are; that worry is futile; that inconveniences mold one into a better man and teach one to appreciate the little things in life.

I'm grateful to the Army for making me gadget conscious; for making useful things out of scraps; for discipline and teamwork, and for the creed of knowing how to take better care of myself!

I'm grateful for the summer I spent at camp where I overcame my fear of water. The councilor left me alone to conquer my fear—and I did in the perfectly natural and normal manner of first wading in the lake and learning that the water could be my ally and not an enemy.

I'm grateful for the summer I spent as an ice cream peddler in the city streets. I downed shyness. I had to use initiative and aggressiveness while plying my trade. I learned that people always aren't out to "bite you!"

I'm grateful to a postal system that brings us weeks closer to home; for the movies and their vivid entertainment; for radio with it's heartening news, and the press for it's diversified reading matter.

I'm grateful to circuses and their conglomeration of all-around eye-filling pleasures. I'm grateful to the scientific world and it's many unsung heroes in research laboratories flung throughout the States who gave us Adrenalin and Sulfanilinide so that the dead might come to life and the wounded given a more than better chance at recovery.

I'm grateful for the expenseless pleasures of a sun bath and the "it's great to be alive" feeling that goes with a brisk walk.

I'm grateful to Uncle Sam for permitting me to serve in his man's Army! Living in close proximity with so many other Americans each stemmed from so many different ancestries is a supreme education in itself... an education that could not be gained elsewhere outside our Armed Forces!

And in conclusion I'm going to be grateful to a powerful nation that already is planning ahead to provide for her fighting men when they return!

Here is a photo of the Camp Amirabad barracks.

Sam wrote an article to describe any soldier that doesn't want to be in military service. It was published in February of 1943.

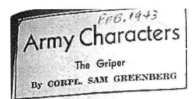

For ease of reading, here is a copy of the article.

Feb. 1943

Army Characters
The Griper
By CORPL. SAM GREENBERG

The Griper is just a Guy who grouses from the time he tumbles out of bunk at reveille until he again hits his bunk at taps!

The bugle bothers him: Its booming notes boisterously bring him to abrupt wakefulness!

His bed mate bothers him: both bunks being too close to each other and oft times the soldiers get their G.I. shoes mixed and the griper gripes!

He's not neat: so he gives vent to noisy nothings when he can't find his necktie!

He beefs about the chilly air upon falling out: but his feeble fault-findings fall on empty ears!

Usually asks some soldier to get broom for sweeping up: then he complains about scarcity of bristles on broom!

While mopping around his bed area, he'll mopingly mutter about how he didn't hafta do any maintenance at home!

Breakfast brings on bumptious bombasts against bad (?) (It's usually good) food!

He puffs with indignation when police-up duties are politely tossed his way and he plunges into puffing patter usually delivered in a pallid undertone!

Marching in formation to school finds him beefing and pitying himself that such a miserable misfit as he should be on moving maneuvers, even though only minutes on way to school!

In the Motor Shop School queries re motors find him quarreling with instructors and ruining lectures with queer questions!

The evening chow line sees him wriggling impatiently with a worried wail like: why keep me waiting for my food!

And so our Griper goes to bed, gripped in gloom, usually glaring at the ceiling until he glimmers off to sleep, because tomorrow reveille will "glow" again!

THE END

This photo shows the remains of a bridge span from the Sassanian Empire. (Also spelled Sasanian and Sassanid/Sasanid.)

The Sasanian Empire ruled from 224 to 651 AD. During Late Antiquity, the Sasanian Empire also recorded as the Sassanian, Sasanid and Sassanid is considered to have been one of Iran's most important, and influential historical periods and constituted the last vast Iranian empire before the Muslim conquest and the adoption of Islam. In many ways, the Sasanian period witnessed the peak of ancient Iranian civilization. The Sasanians' cultural influence extended far beyond the empire's territorial borders, reaching as far as Western Europe, Africa, China, and India.[2]

Sam was in Hamadan, Iran (also spelled Hamedan) and took a picture of an early carving of a lion. Sam said the sculpture was 3,000 years old.

Hamadan is the oldest Iranian city and one of the oldest in the world. While lacking antique vestiges, Hamadan, has several monuments worthy of interest.

A few of the monuments are A Stone Lion: It is the statue of a lion, which was carved out in the Arsacian era, but has now lost the original appearance. The statue is a symbol of the city of Hamadan.

You can also find the Ganjnaameh Tabloids where we find them written in cuneiform and ancient Persian language. We find them engraved on Alvand Mountain, at the very end of the beautiful valley of Abbas Abad. The tabloids ordered carved by Darius the Great and Xerxes, carry the two supplications of Ahura Mazda and the prayer for the preservation of the country.

There you also find the tomb of Baabaa Taher Oryaan, the mystic Iranian poet.[3]

Sam published this group of two line poems in one of the army publications.

Children Pay

Army allowance wage rates soar
If you're a soldier daddy of four.

Plea

Where's that telescopic sight,,
I've got a blind date for tonight,

Cpl. Sam Greenberg

Avicenna was a Persian polymath who is one of the most significant physicians, astronomers, thinkers, and writers of the Islamic Golden Age. We also find him described as the father of early modern medicine.

AUTHENIC TOMB OF AVICENNA — GREATEST IRANIAN SCIENTIST & PHILOSOPHER. LIVED AROUND 1000-A.D. IRAN - 1943 - HAMADAN

His most famous works are The Book of Healing, a philosophical and scientific encyclopedia, and The Canon of Medicine, a medical encyclopedia.

Besides philosophy and medicine, Avicenna's corpus includes writings on astronomy, alchemy, geography, and geology, psychology, Islamic theology, logic, mathematics, physics, and works of poetry.[4]

Here is a copy of a handwritten letter that Sam sent to his family back home on Cross Street, in Philadelphia, Pennsylvania.

In case you have trouble reading Sam's cursive writing, the following is a copy of the excerpt from that letter:

Dated: Thursday, April , 22, 1943, Iran. (Persia)

Coming in again with much love and kisses for you all in Cross St.!

File: Notice in Rural Weekly: "Anyone found near my chicken house at night will be found there next morning!"

"Said James Roosevelt, addressing a meeting in Hollywood,

My father gave me these hints on speech-making: "Be
sincere … be brief … be seated!"

James Roosevelt was President Franklin D. and Eleanor
Roosevelt's oldest son. He was a Democratic congressman,
American businessman, and Marine. He received the Navy
Cross for extraordinary heroism while serving as a Marine
Corps officer during World War II.[5]

The following two photos are of the tomb of Queen Esther and Mordecai in Hamadan, Iran.

We find Esther in the Book of Esther as a Jewish queen of the Persian king Xerxes I, who reigned 486 to 465 BCE. In the narrative, Xerxes I seeks a new wife after his queen, Vashti, refuses to obey him. Xerxes chose Esther for her beauty.

The king's chief advisor, Haman, is offended by Esther's cousin and guardian, Mordecai, and gets permission from the king to have all the Jews in the kingdom killed. Esther foils the plan and wins permission from the king for the Jews to kill their enemies.[6]

Sam's photo shows the entrance to the tomb. As of this writing, you can go to the YouTube.com website and watch a video by "hershel west" titled "Tomb of Mordechai and Esther in Hamedan, Iran." Dated May 18, 2011, the video shows the inside with all its details.

> Mordecai resided in Susa (Shushan or Shoushan), the metropolis of Persia (now Iran). He adopted his orphaned cousin Esther, whom he brought up as if she were his daughter.

> Mordecai discovered a plot of the king's chamberlains to assassinate the king. Because of Mordecai's vigilance, he prevented the plot. The king remembered Mordecai's service in foiling the assassination plot and honored Mordecai by making Mordecai his chief advisor.[7]

Hand written letter dated April 25, 1943. Sam sends along some quotes from Benjamin Franklin.

Again, reprinted for clarity:

Sunday

4/25/43

"Lots of love, hugs and more kisses for mom, pop, Gilda, and Herman! Sunday 4/25/43

Gilda: IMPORTANT. Send along jar of Nu-Fem (or 2) (deodorant) at Sun Rays–in Package under 8 ounces." File: Benjamin Franklin comes through with the following:

"He that hath a trade hath an estate!"

"He is not well bred that cannot bear ill breeding in others!" "The doors of wisdom are never shut!"

"Having been poor is no shame, but being ashamed of it is!"

This is a photo of a small monument of Darius the Great's inscriptions on the highway near the port city of Khorramshahr, Iran.

The monument shown is close to the highway completion done by the U.S. Army.

Darius the Great was the fourth Persian king of the Achaemenid Empire. He ruled the empire at its peak, between 550 and 486 BCE. Darius organized the empire by dividing it into provinces and placing satraps to govern it. He set up Achaemenid coinage as a new uniform monetary system, along with making Aramaic the official language of the empire. He built roads and introduced standard weights and measures. Through these changes, the empire was centralized and unified.[8]

The Persian Corridor was a supply route through Iran into Soviet Azerbaijan by which British aid and American Lend-Lease supplies transferred to the Soviet Union during World War II.[9]

In 1943, 30,000 Americans helped to man the Persian Corridor and 26–34 percent of the supplies sent to the Soviet Union under the Lend-Lease Act went through Iran.[10]

The following is a war correspondent article that Sam published May, 1943. It was entitled "Don't Scoff or Be Stubborn". He was referring to people with large egos who can't face up to the reality that other people can sometimes be right and that we all have differing opinions.

(In my opinion, we should strive to see the bigger picture, regardless of our personal beliefs, and be objective enough to accept it when the end result can be something greater than

Don't Scoff or Be Stubborn
By CORPORAL SAM GREENBERG (in Persia)

"Oh boy, look! . . . a live!"

HALF

our own ideas could produce. Positive things can emerge from what could at first seem negative, such as having to admit someone else's viewpoint has more validity than our own.)

Again, reprinted for clarity.

Don't Scoff or Be Stubborn
By Corporal Sam Greenberg (In Persia)

I sat in a U.S. Army chapel in Iran, thousands of miles from home, listening enthralled to a speech by our chaplain on "sins" and the ways of "sinners."

Two words stuck in my mind: "scoff" and "stubborn." I walked out of the chapel that sunny morning, realizing that people who scoff at this and that and stubborn people are pernicious people.

They're never content to call what's right, right! They toss invidious phrases, doing their best to undermine solidarity. They always sound off with slurring remarks at any sound speech. "Humph," they say. "He ain't so hot!" Never a compliment or a warm word. "What's he ever done," they scoff.

Stubborn, too, they are. Arguing with them is futile. They edge in the last word with a snippy turn of the mouth. They sin in a truly material sense, never actually physical. They're the species who are the first to condone themselves.

A sure cure for scoffers would be a siege in a fox-hole with bullets whining over their heads. They'd soon learn that now was the time for no scoffing, and being stubborn might only direct a bullet to some vulnerable part of their anatomy.

There's the tale of a scoffer which takes place at a cemetery somewhere. A man, who has just placed flowers on a grave, notices a Chinese placing rice on another grave. The man looks on and says: "What time do you expect your friend to come up and eat the rice?"

The Chinese replies with a bland smile: "The same time your friend comes up to smell the flowers!"

Look back over the centuries gone by and in every instance, any inventive genius, who was on the verge of a great discovery, was the target for ridicule, for scorn, for verbal brickbats and a barrage of scoffing for daring to be different! But the inventor always proved to be of "tougher wood" by withstanding all the ridicule and sticking to his beliefs. Beliefs, which in time, would fight through to a new scientific discovery or a new invention.

"The Medical Soldier," a tabloid published by Carlisle Barracks, Carlisle, Pa., runs a gripe feature entitled: 98 Column! In it are printed all kinds of gripes from the soldier personnel. Recently, the column ran a scoffing line from someone who signed himself "Bn. Charlie" which read: "We think the 98 Column stinks." And editor of the column snaps back with reply: "98 Column is made up of grips out of the box in the PX. If you don't like the column, put something good in the box. It's YOUR column, not ours." (Caps are my own!)

Above paragraph contains a powerful idea solution for scoffers. It's easy to scoff and say, "This ain't so hot," but it takes feeling and brains and courage to apply criticisms to a more constructive vein. A scoffer hasn't got what it takes!

Scoffers are never constructive; they're destructive! A kind word from this breed is impossible. Recently, I had a verbal run-in with one of the men in my outfit. His lack of social perception, his inconsiderateness, got the best of me then, and I blasted off at him and said: "I'll bet you wouldn't know how to throw a compliment at anyone, or say a thing was O.K.!" To myself, I added silently, "You're just too damn stubborn!"

Wouldn't this world be a finer place to live in; wouldn't we all get along better with each other if the ones who scoff and the stubborn ones would take size of themselves?

We're at war now! War is destructive, but out of its destructiveness will come greater constructiveness! In spite of scoffers and stubborn people, and just plain sinners, a better will emerge from the postwar era!

HALT

The following is a photo from May, 1943. It appears to be early morning, with Sam about to shave and the soldier on the left soon to play in a baseball game.

"The Troop Shipper"

This war correspondent article was published May 1943. Sam wrote about a soldier's days on the ship over to the Middle East. The salt water and sleeping conditions made for entirely new experiences!

The Troop Shipper
By CORPORAL SAM GREENBURG

SOLDIERS are a tough breed, but the ocean doesn't recognize breeds! Joe and many others on the troop ship forgot to coordinate their stomach reflexes with the ship lurchings caused by King Neptune's playful (?) antics! Result was that hammock fatigue and gurgitation (latrine, head bowed over helmet or hanging over rail style) became the most popular form of diversion the first and second day our ship ploughed through the waters. This Joe hung on to his stomach reflexes!

Warm weather forced many Joes to seek and devise new sleeping quarters! This Joe at times slept on a row of five empty soft drink containers; on elongated box which housed life belts; on deck floors with blankets improvised as mattress; on top of hatch covers or deck; under the protective covering of a mess table, and the good old Navy standby: a hammock. Joe learned how to sleep flat on his back and that G.I. blankets are mighty valuable when pursuing any of above sleeping styles!

Scrubbing detail was welcomed by this Joe in place of all-day K.P. A shovel was used to gather up the excess water on this job.

Most every Joe acquired a taste for peanuts (vitamins A, B & G) and became a tea drinker! Tea and cookies became as familiar as ham and eggs are in the States!

Calisthenics with rifle had Joe following the rifle instead of vice versa, when the ship lurched!

Joe learned how to take a sud-less shower. He'd use soap, but the salt water would never cooperate!

If Joe had the misfortune to soften his beard with salt water, then the safety razor would scratch in vain over beard like a rusty lawn mower rolling over grass. Once, Joe took a semi-salt water shave and at the finish his face looked more in need of a scraping than at the beginning!

One boat drill found Joe and others at their posts, high and dry! Then a few waves got playful and the Joes, staunch in their tracks, were administered quick cold salt water showers.

Sight seeing was taken on the fly. There were flying fishes and school would let out so that schools of fishes could tag along in the ship's wake!

The voyage taught Joe to realize how great is American chow and to appreciate the terra firma!

HALT

For ease of reading, here is a copy of the article.

THE TROOP SHIPPER
By CORPORAL SAM GREENBURG

Soldiers are a tough breed, but the ocean doesn't recognize breeds! Joe and many others on the troop ship forgot to coordinate their stomach reflexes with the ship lurchings caused by King Neptune's playful (?) antics! Result was that hammock fatigue and gurgitation (latrine, head bowed over helmet or hanging over rail style) became the most popular form of diversion the first and second

day our ship ploughed through the waters. This Joe hung
on to his stomach reflexes!

Warm weather forced many Joes to seek and devise
new sleeping quarters! This Joe at times slept on a row of
five empty soft drink containers; on elongated box which
housed life belts; on deck floors with blanket improvised
as mattress; on top of hatch covers or deck; under the
protective covering of a mess table, and the good old
Navy standby: a hammock. Joe learned how to sleep flat
on his back and that G.I. blankets ware mightily valuable
when pursuing any of above sleeping styles!

Scrubbing detail was welcomed by this Joe in place
of all-day K.P. A shovel was to gather up the excess
water on this job.

Most every Joe acquired a taste for peanuts (vitamins
A, B & G) and became a tea drinker! Tea and cookies
became as familiar as ham and eggs are in the States!

Calisthenics with rifle had Joe following the rifle
instead of vice versa, when the ship lurched!

Joe learned how to take a sud-less shower. He'd use
soap, but the salt water would never cooperate!

If Joe had the misfortune to soften his beard with salt
water, then the safety razor would scratch in vain over
beard like a rusty lawn mower rolling over grass. Once,
Joe took a semi-salt water shave and at the finish his face
looked more in need of scraping than at the beginning!

One boat drill found Joe and others at their posts,
high and dry! Then a few waves got playful and the Joes,
staunch in their tracks, were administered quick cold
salt water showers.

Sight seeing was taken on the fly. There were flying
fishes and school would let out so that schools of fishes

could tag along in the ship's wake!

The voyage taught Joe to realize how great is American chow and to appreciate terra firma!

HALT

The photo that follows is a view of The Old Bridge at Dizful, six miles east of Andimeshk, Iran. In 1943, it was spelled Dizful; the spelling has since been changed to Dezful.

The bridge was built during the Sassanid dynasty 1700 years ago by Roman prisoners of war. The bridge is just for civilians; cars are no longer permitted to use the bridge.[11]

"Our Camp Newspaper Editors"

Sam sums it up in this war correspondent article from June 1943. He writes that the printed word builds up the morale of our fighting forces all over the world. He describes the camp newspaper editors, who they are, and where they come from. He says they write news, features, and humor.

The following is a copy of the publication's text.

Our Camp Newspaper Editors
By CORPORAL SAM GREENBERG
(In the Middle East)

Print is not mightier than the sword, but the printed word does a lot to build up the morale of our fighting forces all over the world! And our Soldier-newspaper editors in the Army Camps and out in the field are all knocking out their part in the fighting effort by writing reams of newsy, chatty, pithy humor, swash-buckling sports and powerful editorials. And, of course, advice to the love-lorn, which always goes over big with our Joes.

Our Camp newspaper editors are usually newspapermen, advertising men, radio script writers, trade journal writers or just average guys who always have had a latent ability to write, but never had the chance to express themselves … and then the Army comes along and swoops them up, and these lucky last few wind up writing news, features and humor for some Army sheet.

Our G.I. newspaper editor is an intrepid soul. (We'll skip the soft stuff of putting out a Camp newspaper in the confines of a large training camp in the States!) Nothing should, and nothing does daunt him! With a Special Service publishing kit, he can put out some kind of a sheet or newspaper anywhere under the most difficult of conditions. He doesn't have to worry about a staff, for he alone, if necessary, if willing to work hard, can do a commendable job! Copy always is around when there are fighting men in strange locales, the tasks of improving and bettering your living conditions under trying circumstances and the enemy to contend with!

What greater solace can a Joe find than to see his stuff in print and at the same time camp editors know that many other Joes in his company are going to be entertained and their spirits boosted and their minds dragged away from the cold realities of fighting!

Our Joe (Editor) gets to know everyone! And he gets to printing such Army humor gems (funny enough to cheer up any Soldier) as the following:

Draft Board Doctor to Armless Man: "You're 1–A!"

Armless Man: "But what can I do in the Army?"

D.B.D.:"Don't worry, the Army will find a spot for you!"

Sgt. (to Armless Man) at camp: "Do you see that Soldier over there filling that pail of water?"

Armless Soldier: "Yeah, but what do I do!"

Sgt.: "Well, when the pail becomes full, you tell that soldier to stop! He's blind!"

So come on, Joe, if you write an interesting letter you can write something for your Army sheet!

HALT

This photo's title is "Rebuilt Palace of Queen Ester–25 Miles South of Andimeshk". The rebuilt palace (now Shush Castle) is the structure located in the photo on the horizon. Known in Queen Esther's day as the palace of Shushan, the city now standing down-slope is called Susa.

> Shush Castle is in the ruins of the ancient city of Susa in the Khuzestan Province of Iran. French archaeologist. Jean-Marie Jacques de Morgan in the late 1890s created the Castle. The Castle is similar to medieval monuments in France. The structure built by local craftsmen with bricks taken from two other archaeological sites, the Darius castle and the Elamite Choqazanbil ziggurat.[12]

The two photos on the following page are ruins of a bridge from around 500 A.D. The bridge may have been created by captured Roman engineers and soldiers and the ruins are located south of Khorramabad, Iran.

(19) ANOTHER SHOT OF # 18 -

IRAN - 1943

(18) RUINS OF BRIDGE AROUND 500 A.D.
PERHAPS BY CAPTURED
ROMAN ENGINEERS + SOLDIERS
SOUTH OF KHORRAMABAD

IRAN - 1943

The second golden era (498–622) began after the second
reign of Kavadh I. Kavadh launched a campaign against the
Romans. Kavadh succeeded in restoring order in the interior

and fought with general success against the Eastern Romans, founded several cities, some of which were named after him, and began to regulate taxation and internal administration.[13]

"The U.S.O.'er"

Published June 1, 1943, this article describes personal experiences with the U.S.O. in Atlanta, Georgia, and in Virginia. USO stands for the United Service Organization which was created to support America's service members.

Here is a reprint for clarity.

June 1943

The U.S.O.'er
By CORPORAL SAM GREENBERG

Some guys were always broke before entering the Army! Others, for the first time encountered this financial bugaboo after being clothed in khaki!

What's a guy without a nickel in his jeans, to do? That is where the U.S.O comes in and with it the perennial habitue of the U.S.O., the U.S.O.'er!

Our Joe is busted! He can hitch a ride (against Army Regulations) into town, but his method of approach should never consist of just crude thumbing: Jose should stretch out in the middle of the highway and stop a hop, thusly!

Once in town (Atlanta, Georgia, one of the best Soldier towns in the States), he can get a plentiful stomachful of cakes and coffee at the Service Men's — U.S.O. Center. Between reading a varied assortment of magazines and listening to strains of a juke box, he can sign up for a Sunday dinner (with private family) and attend Church services, also!

If dining at a friendly home doesn't please him. Joe can walk out to the K. of C. Here he can put on the feed bag or step on some femme feet while dancing!

At the terminal train station the U.S.O Center is run by women, who are tops with looks, charm, and friendliness. Joe, up on his first visit, tried to date up all of the hostesses even though they scored a few years on him. Joe can walk in here, his stomach flat as a stingy chef's pancake, and later toddle out, a well-fed Soldier.

In between times, our Joe can stare himself goffle-eyed by gazing at the Pulchritudinous Flow of Peachtree Street Womanhood.

Some days Joe can dance with gals dressed in evening gowns; he can hop to juke box tunes; and on Friday nights he can relaxedly watch professional wrestlers exhibit their many mangling antics of mayhem on the mat!

Also, Joe can tell about the time he visited U.S.O. in Virginia. Being Atlanta trained, he asked about getting a "FREE MEAL." And the gal in charge in retort replied: "Sorry but there are no "FEMALES" available!"

HALT

One of Sam's V-mails was published in the magazine Modern
Romances, July 1943.

> V-mail was short for Victory Mail. It was how soldiers in
> World War II communicated with a person back in the
> United States. The V-mail letter was hand written or typed
> by the soldier then censored by the military service, after
> which it was microfilmed and sent back to the States. Once
> arriving back in the U.S., it was blown up and reprinted,
> then sent to the designated address. This process reduced
> the cost of transferring an original letter through the military
> postal system.[14]

The first scan is from Sam's scrapbook showing the V-mail that they
published in the July 1943 issue. In that scan, you can see the letter
sent by the editor of Modern Romances, Hazel L. Berge. His published
letter of the comment earned him $5. The second scanned image is
the front cover of the July 1943 issue that I purchased on eBay.

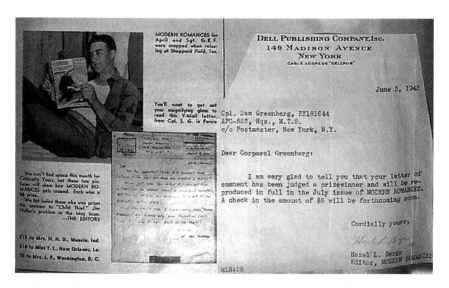

The following is a copy of Sam's V-mail.

Sir,

The two uppermost things in a soldier's mind (outside of the war) are Home and Romance, I believe!

We've just seen two motion pictures out here in Iran (on an outdoor screen) in inclement weather, but how we enjoyed our nearness to a bit of the romantic United States.

Even though a man, I occasionally read "Modern Romances" and wonder why your magazine can't find its way to this part of the earth!

Sincerely,

cpl. Sam Greenberg

The following is a copy of the letter from Dell Publishing.

```
The Dell Publishing Company, Inc.
149 Madison Avenue
New York
Cable Address "Dellpub"
```

June 3, 1943
Cpl. Sam Greenberg, 33181644
Apo_523, Hqs., M.T.S.
c/o Postmaster, New York, N.Y.

Dear Corporal Greenberg:

I am very glad to tell you that your letter of comment has been judged a prizewinner and will be reproduced in full in the July issue of MODERN ROMANCES. A check in the amount of $5 will be forthcoming soon.

Cordially yours,
Hazel L. Berge
Editor, Modern Romances

Here is a scan of the July 1943 issue of "Modern Romances" that I found and purchased from the internet.

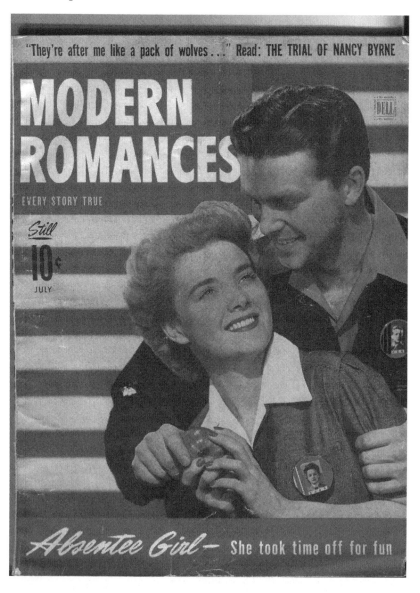

This is a photo of Khorramabad, a city in western Iran. The mountains in the background are the Lorestan mountains, part of the Zagros Mountain range. Farther back, the castle on the right is Falak-ol-Aflak Castle.

We find this gigantic structure built during the Sassanid era (224–651).[15]

This is a recent close-up photo of Falak-ol-Aflak Castle.

Photo by Omid.koli, CC BY-SA 3.0,

The following article was published July 1943, requesting that all Motor Transport Service personnel create a needed device and market it. This was something my father always wanted to do. He kept a small book for ideas and inventions.* Many years later, I was surprised and happy to find this book among things my dad left to me. I remembered seeing it in my early days and how excited and inspired I always was, looking through the small book.

Pictures, Stories May Mean Bucks

Attention MTS Personnel: Various auto and trade journals in several states (check for. addresses with Special Service) pay real money for gadget items and photos. Have you or any of your buddies worked up a gadget to remedy some kink in your everyday work? Write it up briefly; if no picture, work up a pen and ink illustration of the labor saving device and submit!

Mechanix Illustrated, 1501 Broadway, New York, N.Y. is on the lookout for items for use in "Ideas for Service Men" department.

Have any of you Joes built a unique hanger, ash tray, cabinet or what have you? If so, look around for a market. Somebody will buy it.

Cpl. Sam Greenberg, MTS

The following V-Mail was titled "Persian Privy" It shows an illustration of a Persian privy which is a toilet of the outhouse variety. He first talks of the greatest of all Persian poets, Omar Khayyam, then of the American poet, James Whitcomb Riley who may have written a poem called "The Passing of the Outhouse," although Sam calls it "The Passing of the Back House." It was never published in Riley's collection of poetry.

---

* See My Dad's Book of Ideas at the end of *Somewhere in Persia* for a few examples of his ideas.

At the end of this V-Mail, Sam rewrites some of the end lines of that poem. This V-Mail was written on Aug. 11, 1943.

Omar Khayyam was a Persian mathematician, astronomer, and poet. Most of his life was the period which witnessed the First Crusade. He was born on May 18, 1048 and died December 4, 1131.[16]

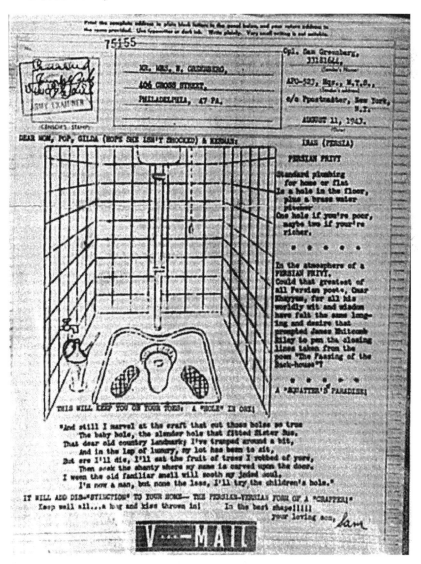

The following is a copy of the V-mail text.

Iran (Persia)
Dear Mom, Pop, Gilda (Hope She Isn't Shocked) &
Herman,

          Persian Privy

Standard plumbing
    for home or flat
Is a hole in the floor,
    plus a brass water pitcher
One hole if you're poor,
    maybe two if you're richer.

          ★ ★ ★ ★ ★

In the atmosphere of a PERSIAN PRIVY.

Could that greatest of all Persian poets, Omar
Khayyam, for all his worldly wit and wisdom have
felt the same longing and desire that prompted
James Whitcomb Riley to pen the lines taken from
the poem "The Passing of the Back House"?

          ★ ★ ★ ★ ★

    A SQUATTER'S PARADISE! THIS WILL KEEP YOU ON
          YOUR TOES, A "HOLE" IN ONE!

"And still I marvel at the craft that cut those
holes so true,
    The baby's hole, and the slender hole that
    fitted Sister Sue,

That dear old country landmark; I tramped around
a bit,

   And in the lap of luxury my lot has been to sit,
But ere I die I'll eat the fruits of trees I
robbed of yore,

   Then seek the shanty where my name is carved
   upon the door.
I ween that old familiar smell will sooth my jaded
soul,

   I'm now a man, but none the less I'll try the
   children's hole."

   IT WILL ADD DIS-"STINCTION" TO YOUR HOME-- THE
     PERSIAN-VERSIAN FORM OF A "CRAPPER"

Keep well all a hug and kiss thrown in!

             In the best shape!!!!!
               your loving son,
                   Sam

"Pesky Trucklins Gum Up Works for Motor Transport Service Boys"

The article is full of humor and creative dialect. He even writes of Gremlins long ago who "gave geezer, Darius, plenty of trouble when he was pushing around his chariot." The "Trucklins" were half-cousins of the "Gremlins" of RAF and USAAF fame. The article was published on Aug. 29, 1943.

Pesky Trucklins Gum Up Works For Motor Transport Service Boys

Hey, Joe didja see those posters on the "Trucklins!" There's "Benny," an oldster. He's the guy who gives us MTS truckers aches and pains in the kidneys, while we're hauling all that stuff up to the Russians. There's "Barney Oldfeet," a pesky little sonofagun, with an extra large left hand and long arm for pushing down on our accelerator foot when we shouldn't.

Didja ever notice that hitch-hiker, the "Cowboy Trucklin," who spots us sometimes a mile away and snitches a ride on our cab as we tear along, when we oughta take it easy. And Joe, I know we all like femme company, so watch out for that siren of the road, Dinah Shorinella, a female "Trucklin," who will sing us to sleep at the wheel, wheedle us into parking in the middle of a road or on blind corners, and if she gets a chance, lull us into a false sense of security and cause plenty of damn-fool accidents. So watch out for her, Joe.

These pesky "Trucklins" half-cousins of the "Gremlins" of RAF and USAAF fame—have jumped some of us MTS truckers and hoodwinked plenty of us into accidents while carting cargo North for use by the Russians.

That Pfc. Edward Greene got a great brainstorm when he thought up this one. Greene, a member of a trucking outfit down the line, clicked with these trouble-making small folk, when the Accident Bureau of MTS asked for ideas as part of their Safety Campaign Drive.

These "Trucklins", Joe, even gave that geezer, Darius plenty of trouble when he was pushin' his chariot around here, years ago (and pushin' other people around too)...they'd keep pulling splinters out of his wooden tires and loosen all the nuts and bolts... just when the going was toughest.

Cpl. Sam Greenberg, MTS

The following is a copy of Sam's publication.

Pesky Trucklins Gum Up Works For Motor Transport Service Boys

Hey, Joe didja see those posters on the "Trucklins!" There's "Benny," an oldster. He's the guy who gives us MTS truckers aches and pains in the kidneys, while we're hauling all that stuff up to the Russians. There's "Barney Oldfeet," a pesky little sonofagun, with an extra large left hand and long arm for pushing down on our accelerator foot when we shouldn't.

Didja ever notice that hitch-hiker, the "Cowboy Trucklin." who spots us sometimes a mile away and snitches a ride on our cab as we tear along, when we oughta take it easy. And Joe, I know we all like femme company, so watch out for that siren of the road, Dinah Shorinella, a female "Trucklin," who will sing us to sleep at the wheel, wheedle us into parking in the middle of a road or on blind corners, and if she gets a chance, lull us into a false sense of security and cause plenty of damn-fool accidents. So watch out for her, Joe.

These pesky "Trucklins" half-cousins of the "Gremlins" of RAF and USAAF fame—have jumped some of us MTS truckers and hood-winked plenty of us into accidents while carting cargo North for use by the Russians.

That Pfc. Edward Greene got a great brainstorm when he thought up this one. Greene, a member of a trucking outfit down the line, clicked with these trouble-making small folk, when the Accident Bureau of MTS asked for ideas as part of their Safety Campaign Drive.

These "Trucklins", Joe, even gave that geezer, Darius plenty of trouble when he was pushin' his chariot around here, years ago (and pushin' other people around too)… they'd keep pulling splinters out of his wooden tires and loosen all the nuts and bolts… just when the going was toughest.

Cpl. Sam Greenberg, MTS

Sam only took two photos depicting the convoys carrying supplies to Russia. Even though these two photos have blemishes, I chose to use them in this book.

"Sgt. Patrick Knows His Tree Frogs Well"

Published September 12, 1943, Sam writes about Pvt. Pat Chesley
of West Liberty, Kentucky, who worked as a guard all night in the
generator plant. Pat talked to Sam about the difference between the
Iraqi tree frogs and the Kentucky swamp frogs. Read the article to
find what Pat misses most from civilian life. This article was published
Sept. 12, 1943.

Sept. 12,43. DISPATCH

Sgt. Patrick Knows His Tree Frogs Well

Sounds in the night keep Pvt. Chesley (Pat) Patrick, of West Liberty, Kentucky, company during his lonely vigil as guard all night in the light generator plant close to the Post Dispensary, Amirabad.

The croakings of tree frogs put Patrick into a reminiscent mood as he closely watches the complicated 4800 watt generator with its maze of knobs, ampere and voltage meters and regulators from 6:30 p.m. This generator supplies electric lights for most of the Post during these hours.

"Tree frogs," drawled Patrick, a veteran soldier, "are different from the U.S. species. They have a 2 inch tail, sharp claws and are four to five inches long with a greenish-brown body. Their croaking is all done in a tree which they climb easily. Boy, they sure do remind me of good ole Kentucky, with it's swamp frogs. And maybe I don't have plenty of time during the quiet work hours to think of the fishing I'm missing and the lack of a bird season and rabbit hunting in Iran."

"Baby Burro Goes All GI"

Sam writes about their mascot, Susie and how she participates in the softball games at MTS Station No.1. It was published in September of 1943.

Baby Burro Goes All GI

That pet baby burro at MTS Station No. 1 now sports an MTS work button on its leather neck-collar and has the letters MTS (three and one-half inches in height) clipped out on both sides of its furry coat. During softball games in which MTS participates, the burro wears a coat (just like the famous Army mule) with sign on both sides in vari-colors: HQS. MTS—WE KICK, BUT WE "KEEP" EM ROLLING".

Cpl. Sam Greenberg, MTS

Susie Gobbles Dance Spotlight 9/19/43

"Susie," the baby burro mascot of MTS Station No. 1, stole the show at the MTS-61st QM Laundry dance last Saturday night at Rec Hall No. 1. Susie rode to the dance in a truck driven by Cpl. Wenzel of Rapid City, S.D.

Led through the door to the the hall, Susie tried the dance floor, and then retired to the doorway, where she held the spotlight for the evening, even attracting more attention than the girls who came for the dance.

Cpl. Sam Greenberg

"Susie Gobbles Dance Spotlight"

A short article about Susie the baby burro mascot of MTS (Motor Transport Service) Station Number 1. This article published on September 19, 1943.

Sunday, Sept. 20, 1943, a day after Saturday's dance, just before a swim.

V-Mail Sam sent home to his family in Philadelphia, Pennsylvania on Sept. 25, 1943. It was a greeting for the Jewish holiday Rosh Hashanah from Persia.

Rosh Hashanah is known as the Jewish New Year. In 1943, the Jewish year was 5704.

> Rosh Hashanah is a two-day celebration that begins on the first day of Tishrei, which is the seventh month of the ecclesiastical year. It includes attending synagogue services and reciting special liturgy about teshuva, as well as enjoying festive meals.[17]

> Teshuva means repentance and is one element of atoning for sin in Judaism.[18]

"Yom Kippur Eve–Iran 1943"

The first photo is from Sept. 29, 1943. Sam can be seen under the middle check mark.

YOM KIPPUR EVE - IRAN - 1943

The second photo was taken the next day, September 30. It was taken during a Yom Kippur service at camp with the blowing of the shofar.

For those unfamiliar with Yom Kippur, it is the most important holiday of the Jewish year. Yom Kippur means Day of Atonement.

Yom Kippur is the holiest day of the year in Judaism. Its central themes are atonement and repentance. Jewish people traditionally observe this Blessed day with an approximate 25-hour period of fasting and intensive prayer, often spending most of the day in synagogue services.[19]

"Desert District Plans Extensive Sports Program"

The first sentence says: "Keep 'em in shape for any rough stuff that might come along". The enlisted men played sports to help them stay in shape, organizing and playing volleyball, basketball, football and baseball. The article was published on Oct. 3, 1943.

Here is a reprint for clarity.

10/3/43

Desert District Plans Extensive Sports Program

"Keep 'em in shape for any rough stuff that might come along".

That will be the key note of the of the athletic training program now in formation for personnel of Hq. Co., declared Pvt. John A. Unick, of North Braddock, PA., who is physical director of the set-up.

1st Lt. Vincent P. Donohue, commanding officer, picked Unick because of his outstanding athletic ability in high school and college.

10/3/43

Desert District Plans Extensive Sports Program

"Keep 'em in shape for any rough stuff that might come along".

That will · be the key note of the athletic training program now in formation for personnel of Hq. Co., declared Pvt. John A. Unick, of North Braddock, Pa., who is physical director of the set-up.

1st Lt. Vincent P. Donohue, commanding officer, picked Unick because of his outstanding athletic ability in high school and college.

Unick is encouraging inter-billet games of volley ball and basket ball. He also is organizing a touch football team of MTS men.

Made All state

In high school Unick, playing end and then switching to right half back, was chosen all-state in his junior year. He landed on the all-opponent team for two years running in basketball. His activities then covered 1936 to 1938.

During the recently closed softball season at Amirabad, Unick was star pitcher for the MTS team. At present he is a pitcher and outfielder on the all-star team of the Post.

Unick is encouraging inter-billet games of volley ball and basket ball. He also is organizing a touch football team of MTS men.

Made All State

In high school Unick, playing end and then switching to right half back, was chosen all-state in his junior year. He landed on the all-opponent team for two years running in basketball. His activities then covered 1936 to 1938.

During the recently closed softball season at Amirabad. Unick was star pitcher for the MTS team. At present he is a pitcher and outfielder on the all-star team of the Post.

"Former Coal Miner Had Two Narrow Escapes From Death"

The private was asked the question as to whether he would be inclined to show fear if he was thrown into actual combat. He replied, "I don't know." He did talk about two near-death experiences that he had while mining coal in 1940 to 1941. The publication date was Oct. 10, 1943.

Former Coalminer Had Two Narrow Escapes From Death

"I don't know" Two narrow escapes from death underground while mining coal in 1940 and 1941 provided the reply for Pfc. Charles S. Klimasheski of Hq. Co. MTS. in answer to a question as to whether he would be inclined to show fear if he was thrown into actual combat.

Klimasheski, now an auto mechanic's helper, experienced fear when he was tossed ten feet through the air and stunned against the rib of a tunnel when caught in a gas explosion in 1941. He was working in an old mine in Shamokin, Pa. 300 feet underground and a spark from a dynamite detonator touched off some gas in the air.

In 1940 this same soldier miner had a close call when carbon monoxide fumes almost trapped him in the same mine.

How do miners detect gas? Detection is accomplished by carrying an oil lamp which has a fine mesh screen to keep out air. Gas is lighter than air, and if there is gas in the underground pocket, the flame in the lamp grows larger and then goes out. At the first sign of a swelling flame, the miner should beat a hasty retreat, don a gas mask and go back with a compressed air gun to spray the area.

After the war Klimasheski intends to go back to structural steel work, which he claims is less hazardous than mining. Between cracks at coal mining, he worked as a bucker and riveter on construction jobs.

Cpl Sam Greenberg

I have retyped for clarity.

10/10/43 — Dispatch

Former Coalminer Had Two Narrow Escapes From Death

"I don't know"

Two narrow escapes from death underground while mining coal in 1940 and 1941 provided the reply for Pfc. Charles S. Klimasheski of Hq. Co. MTS in answer to a question as to whether he would be inclined to show fear if he was thrown into actual combat.

Klimasheski, now an auto mechanic's helper, experienced fear when he was tossed ten feet through the air and stunned against the rib of a tunnel when caught in a gas explosion in 1941. He was working in an old mine in Shamokin, Pa. 300 feet underground and a spark from a dynamite detonator touched off some gas in the air.

In 1940 this same soldier miner had a close call when carbon monoxide fumes almost trapped him in the same mine.

How do miners detect gas? Detection is accomplished by carrying an oil lamp which has a fine mesh screen to keep out air. Gas is lighter than air, and if there is gas in the underground pocket, the flame in the lamp grows larger and then goes out. At the first sign of a swelling flame, the miner should beat a hasty retreat, don a gas mask and go back with a compressed air gun to spray the area.

After the war Klimasheski intends to go back to structural steel work, which he claims is less hazardous than mining. Between cracks at coal mining, he worked as a bucker and riveter on construction jobs.

Cpl. Sam Greenberg

"Joseph's French Horn Will Sound Again When Adolph Bites Dust"

Private Joseph Podlaski from Brooklyn, New York, made a vow not to play the French horn again until Nazism was wiped off the face of the earth. He was a truck driver. It was published Oct. 17, 1943.

UNITED STATES ARMY DISPATCH

Joseph's French Horn Will Sound Again When Adolph Bites Dust

In September, 1939, the Nazi hordes invaded and conquered Poland. In Brooklyn, N. Y., Joseph Podlaski made a vow not to play the French horn until Nazism was wiped off the face of the earth.

Today, Podlaski, a private with Hq. Co. MTS as truck driver, only gets a desire to "blow it out" on the horn whenever he passes close to the barracks where the Post band is practicing. But the urge wears off, and he has religiously stuck to his pledge.

"When the Nazis are licked", he says with a twinkle in his eye, "I'll go back to my horn".

Born in the States of Polish parents, Podlaski volunteered from New York State for service in the Polish army, training in Canada in 1941. He spent four months learning the intricacies of the light machine gun and four months with medium tanks. After this stretch he asked for and received an honorable discharge.

When called by Uncle Sam Pvt. Podlaski, father of a two-and one-half year baby girl, did not wind up in a branch of service wich might utilize his previous military training. Due to his civilian experience, the Army decided that he would be more valuable as a truck driver.

The MTS trucker has post-war plans all mapped out. Formerly a lead caster with a Brooklyn company, he expects to go back to his trade after the Allies lick the pants off the Axis. And some evenings will be devoted to tooting peacefully on the french horn.

Cpl. Sam Greenberg

The following is a copy of Sam's publication.

UNITED STATES ARMY DISPATCH

10/17/1943

Joseph's French Horn Will Sound Again When Adolph Bites Dust

In September, 1939, the Nazi hordes invaded and conquered Poland. In Brooklyn, N.Y., Joseph Podlaski made a vow not to play the French horn until Nazism was wiped off the face of the earth.

Today, Podlaski, a private with Hq. Co. MTS as truck driver, only gets a desire to "blow it out" on the horn whenever he passes close to the barracks where the Post band is practicing. But the urge wears off, and he has religiously stuck to his pledge.

"When the Nazis are licked", he says with a twinkle in his eye, "I'll go back to my horn".

Born in the States of Polish parents, Podlaski volunteered from New York State for service in the Polish army, training in Canada in 1941. He spent four months learning the intricacies of the light machine gun and four months with medium tanks. After this stretch he asked for and received an honorable discharge.

When called by Uncle Sam Pvt. Podlaski, father of a two and one half year baby girl, did not wind up in a branch of service which might utilize his previous military training. Due to his civilian experience, the Army decided that he would be more valuable as a truck driver.

The MTS trucker has post-war plans all mapped out. Formerly a lead caster with a Brooklyn company, he expects to go back to his trade after the Allies lick the pants off the Axis. And some evenings will be devoted to tooting peacefully on the French horn.

Cpl. Sam Greenberg

"Great Gate of a Ruined Palace at Kazvin–built around 1540 AD"

The city today is known as Qazvin. It is thought to have been founded by Shapur II, King of Persia in 250 CE.[20]

"MTS Celebrates 1st Anniversary"

Sam gives the details of the MTS's first anniversary celebration. It was published Oct. 17, 1943.

Lieutenant Colonel John A. Murphy was the C.O., or commanding officer. This photo shows him feeding Susie at the MTS's anniversary celebration. Susie had a great life for the few years the soldiers were stationed there in Iran. The cake on the lower right, a devil's food cake with chocolate icing, was made for the celebration.

MTS Celebrates 1st Anniversary

The first anniversary of Headquarters Company, MTS, was celebrated Wednesday night in the company mess hall, with a banquet. The outfit was activated at Camp Lee, Va., Oct. 9, 1942.

Speakers were Lt. Col. Sidney Grunieck, executive officer of MTS, representing Col. Glenn Ward, acting director of MTS; Lt. Col. John A. Murphy, commanding officer of MTS No. 1; Capt. David R. Webster, Major William I. Welch and Capt. Clement V. Burns.

Cpl. Lew Levy was toastmaster and T/Sgt. Raymond F. Fahy was chairman of the committee. Chaplain James Murphy was a guest. First Lt. Vincent F. Donohue is commanding officer of Headquarters Company.

Cpl. Sam Greenberg.

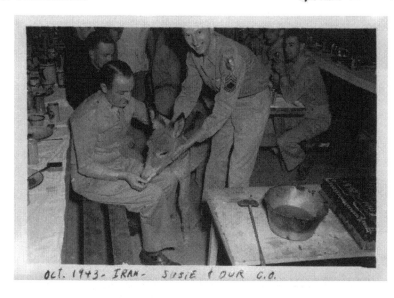

Oct. 1943 - IRAN - SUSIE & OUR C.O.

"Here's a GI Cookie Who Knows When a Soldier Wins at Craps"

This short story is about Corporal Joseph Golden of Brooklyn, N.Y., who started as a driver and became the cook in the mess hall at M.T.S.

UNITED STATES ARMY DISPATCH

Here's a GI Cookie Who Knows When a Soldier Wins at Craps

A cook dishes out the chow in the mess hall and doesn't get around much, but he sure knows who cleaned out the crap game day after payday; or when the fellows get mail..

How? By simply observing the soldiers as they file by for their GI grub.

One such observant Joe is Cpl. Joseph Golden of Hq. Co., MTS, of Brooklyn, N. Y., a pastry cook in civilian life, has a burning ambition. He's a grateful soul, and wants to bake a wedding cake for Sgt. Manuel Rodriguez of Bristol, R.I., who taught the corporal all he knows about the Army culinary art.

The biggest cooking thrill for Golden came recently when he baked a delicious devil's food chocolate covered cake for the banquet commemorating the first anniversary of the formation of the Motor Transport Service.

For a few months Golden was on detached service down the road with an MTS driving school, but not as a cook. He remembers the first truck convoy, and how he drove his first semi-trailer, his only difficulty being in shifting gears, and that not often.

"Tough cooking assignments," relates this jovial-faced GI. "were on our trip across country on a troop train. We had to strap down all the pots to avoid getting our fingers in the food, and had to use splash covers. Those days reminded me of some of the slap-stick scenes we see in movie comedies," said the Brooklynite as he made with appropriate gestures.

"On arriving in Iran we cooks had our troubles. No lights, so we used lanterns and if there was no water in our mess quarters, we had to walk over a quarter-mile to the other mess and lug back the aqua in five-gallon cans.

"I'm glad to be with the boys," emphatically declared Golden, a hefty individual. "Now I can try to fatten 'em up again — not that they need it."

Cpl. Sam Greenberg.

I have retyped for clarity.

10/24/43 United States Army Dispatch

Here's a GI Cookie Who Knows When a Soldier Wins at Craps

A cook dishes out the chow in the mess hall and doesn't get around much, but he sure knows who cleaned out the crap game day after payday; or when the fellows get mail.

How? By simply observing the soldiers as they file by for their GI grub.

One such observant Joe is Cpl. Joseph Golden of Hq. Co., MTS, of Brooklyn, N.Y., a pastry cook in civilian life, has a burning ambition. He's a grateful soul, and wants to bake a wedding cake for Sgt. Manuel Rodriguez of Bristol, R.I., who taught the corporal all he knows about the Army culinary art.

The biggest cooking thrill for Golden came recently when he baked a delicious devil's food chocolate covered cake for the banquet commemorating the first anniversary of the formation of the Motor Transport Service.

For a few months Golden was on detached service down the road with an MTS driving school, but not as a cook. He remembers the first truck convoy, and how he drove his first semi-trailer, his only difficulty being in shifting gears, and that not often.

"Tough cooking assignments," relates the jovial-faced GI, "were on our trip across country on a troop train. We had to strap down all the pots to avoid getting our fingers in the food, and had to use splash covers. Those days reminded me of some of the slap-stick scenes we see in movie comedies," said the Brooklynite as he made with appropriate gestures.

"On arriving in Iran we cooks had our troubles. No lights, so we used lanterns and if there was no water in our mess quarters, we had to walk over a quarter-mile to the other mess and lug back the aqua in five-gallon cans.

"I'm glad to be with the boys," emphatically declared Golden, a hefty individual. "Now I can try to fatten 'em up again—not that they need it."

Cpl. Sam Greenberg.

"The Typewriter Commando!"

Sam adds his own poetry to that of W. R. Delabar. In addition to documenting the unit's time in Iran, Sam was a clerk in charge of the supplies sent to Russia. It was November 1943 and Sam had not done any fighting yet. The Germans never got to the Middle East from the west in North Africa, nor from the north through Russia.

The Typewriter Commando!

"Oh, I just dread the coming of the day
When I will have to hear my children
    say:
Daddy, were you an aviator in the War?
Or did you chase the Germans with a
    tank?
Or were you on the Lexington when it
    sank?
And I'll have to confess, 'I was no daring
    fighter!
Instead, I merely operated a typewriter!'
But wait a happy thought occurs to me
Whereby I may retain my dignity.
I'll say to them, "Oh, I was quite a guy,
I ran a machine and made it fly.
And the number of enemies that I slew
Would be impossible for me to tell to you
But I was a rough, tough, so-and-so
For I was a Service Commando!
            —W. R. Delabar.

• • •

SOME one has to do the paper work in the Army, so our Typewriter Commando shouldn't feel too bad because he isn't out there shouldering a rifle and knocking off a few Nazis and Japs. His is the job to do all his banging on a typewriter!

But our Joe has other ideas about waging war!

Our Joe, the Typewriter Commando, instead of typing a report, would like to hear some artillery retort!

Instead of drafting a chart, he'd like to be in a battle's start!

Instead of messing around filing cabinets, he'd like to be one soldier behind a line of bayonets!

He'd like to engage in a withering enfilade, instead of maybe worrying about a military grade!

Cast off A.R. (Army Regulations) on who gets paid, and engage in an enemy raid!

Be part of a land force invasion, instead of dabbling with division!

Our Typewriter Commando would like to engage in a foraging fray, instead of just going through another typing day!

He's tired of polite office speech, and would like to hear a shell's screech!

He's bored with bending over office blanks, and would like to engage in a battle of tanks!

Give him some spirited military feints, instead of correspondence complaints!

Give him a chance to kill instead of close order drill!

Give him a chance to give vent to a curse, instead of a typewriter to nurse!

No more facts to cite, but a chance to fight! He'd like to engage in some enemy's routs, and thus get away from some correspondence doubts!

So buck up, Joe, there's no telling when the time may come, when you can chuck your typewriter and let your fingers manipulate a gun!
            —Corporal Sam Greenberg (In Persia)

In case you have trouble reading the scan of Sam's article, the following is a retype of its text.

The Typewriter Commando!

"Oh, I just dread the coming of the day
When I will have to hear my children say:
Daddy, were you an aviator in the War?
Or did you chase the Germans with a tank?
Or were you on the Lexington when it sank?
And I'll have to confess, 'I was no daring fighter!
Instead I merely operated a typewriter!'

But wait a happy thought occurs to me
Whereby I may retain my dignity.
I'll say to them, "Oh, I was quite a guy,
I ran a machine and made it fly.
And the number of enemies that I slew
Would be impossible for me to tell to you
But I was a rough, tough, so-and-so
For I was a Service Commando!

—W.R. Delabar.

★ ★ ★

Some one has to do the paper work in the Army, so our Typewriter Commando shouldn't feel too bad because he isn't out there shouldering a rifle and knocking off a few Nazis and Japs. His is the job to do all his banging on a typewriter!

But our Joe has other ideas about waging war!

Our Joe, the Typewriter Commando, instead of typing a report would like to hear some artillery retort!

Instead of drafting a chart, he'd like to be in a battle's start!

Instead messing around filing cabinets, he'd like to be one soldier behind a line of bayonets!

He'd like to engage in a withering enfilade, instead of maybe worrying about a military grade!

Cast off A.R. (Army Regulations) on who gets paid, and engage in an enemy raid!

Be part of a land force invasion, instead of dabbling with division!

Our Typewriter Commando would like to engage in a foraging fray, instead of just going through another typing day!

He's tired of polite office speech, and would like to hear a shell's screech!

He's bored with bending over office blanks, and would like to engage in a battle of tanks!

Give him some spirited military feints, instead of correspondence complaints!

Give him a chance to kill instead of close order drill!

Give him a chance to give vent to a curse, instead of a typewriter to nurse!

No more facts to cite, but a chance to fight! He'd like to engage in some enemy's routs, and thus get away from some correspondence doubts!

So buck up, Joe, there's no telling when the time may come, when you can chuck your typewriter and let your fingers manipulate a gun!

—*Corporal Sam Greenberg (In Persia)*

It says in photo #20 that it is the alleged tomb of Daniel, located 25 miles south of Andimeshk, Iran. Daniel was a Jewish prophet. He was well known for interpreting dreams.

In photo #23 you can see some of the mounds covering the ruins of ancient Shush, Iran.

The modern Iranian town of Shush found on the site of ancient Susa is identified as Shushan, mentioned in the Book of Esther and other Biblical books. The site consists of three gigantic mounds, occupying an area of about one square kilometer, known as the Apadana mound, the Acropolis mound, and the Ville Royale (royal town) mound.[21]

"GI Wagers Nazis Will be Defeated by January First."

Corporal Francis McDuffie was a gambling man. He wagered $500 in various bets that the Nazis would be defeated by January 1st, 1944. He based his fortunes on economics.

GI Wagers Nazis Will be Defeated By January First

By the first of January, 1944, Germany will be licked and out of the war, predicts Cpl. Francis H. McDuffie, of a PGSC Army Exchange Unit, of Waterloo, N. Y. And the Corporal backs his beliefs with cold cash in the amount of five hundred real American dollars, with bets all covered by the doubting doughboys who frequent the PX.

McDuffie, (bet he's one of the guys who tells you no rials in change and you walk out of the PX with etc.) was an operations manager for a large mail order house in the States. In this capacity he studied local economic conditions and learned to look ahead in order to advise his employers about the feasibilities of conducting credit business in that section.

Cpl. Mcduffie has one wager for one hundred dollars and the rest in smaller bets of 12,800 rials. He's a thinking man, and he has his own reasons for putting his dollars on the line.

"As soon as the Germans started to lose", declared the soldier sage and amateur 'economist, "their mark began to sink in valued. Right now it is lower on the world money market than at the time of their defeat in the last war! I believe that all wars eventually narrow down to economic wars and further Allied victories will bring about the economic collapse of Germany and her subsequent defeat".

"Look back over the war events of the past three months, analyze them closely, and with the present victorious Allied trend, we'll surely win in two months", McDuffie opined between sips of beer. "Huge amounts of troops don't mean a thing if there isn't a solid financial structure to back them. The Germans have bled the conquered countries of all their resources so that the money of these countries is valueless on the world exchange today!"

Cpl. James Gorby, of the same outfit, who covered the hundred dollar wager, told McDuffie "This is one bet I'll be glad to lose".

McDuffie intends to plunk his entire winnings into War Bonds!

(Cpl. Sam Greenberg)

Again, reprinted for clarity.

11/1/43

GI Wagers Nazis Will be Defeated by January First

By the first of January 1944, Germany will be licked and out of the war, predicts Cpl. Francis H. McDuffie of a PGSC Army Exchange Unit, of Waterloo, N.Y.

And the Corporal backs his beliefs with cold cash in the amount of five hundred real American dollars, with bets all covered by the doubting doughboys who frequent the PX.

McDuffie, (bet he's one of the guys who tells you no rials in change and you walk out of the PX with, etc.) was an operations manager for a large mail order house in the States. In this capacity he studied local economic conditions and learned to look ahead in order to advise his employers about the feasibilities of conducting credit business in that section.

Cpl. McDuffie has one wager for one hundred dollars and the rest in smaller bets of 12,800 rials. He's a thinking man, and he has his own reasons for putting his dollars on the line.

"As soon as the Germans started to lose", declared the soldier sage and amateur economist, "their mark began to sink in value. Right now it is lower on the world money market than at the time of their defeat in the last war! I believe that all wars eventually narrow down to economic wars and further Allied victories will bring about the economic collapse of Germany and her subsequent defeat".

"Look back over the war events of the past three months, analyze them closely, and with the present victorious Allied trend, we'll surely win in two months", McDuffie opined between sips of beer. "Huge amounts of troops don't mean a thing if there isn't a solid financial structure to back them. The Germans have bled the conquered countries of all their resources so that the money of these countries is valueless on the world exchange today!"

Cpl. James Gorby, of the same outfit, who covered the hundred dollar wager, told McDuffie "This is one bet I'll be glad to lose".

McDuffie intends to plunk his entire winnings into War Bonds!

(Cpl. Sam Greenberg)

"Susie Needs Pair of Shoes But MTS Gang Won't Depend on Crap Game."

Susie was native to the area, and was taken in by the boys of MTS headquarters. After being well-fed and spoiled by the men, she looked like an entirely different animal.

Susie Needs Pair of Shoes But MTS Gang Won't Depend on Crap Game

Susie, a native of Persia was adopted several months ago by the boys of MTS headquarters. She was then typical of the country—thin and emaciated, and didn't have any shoes.

The MTS gang took good care of Susie. Under the careful eyes of GI dieticians, she has filled out admirably. Her ribs are no longer visible through her skin, and her body is filled out perfectly so that now she is among the finest of her type.

Naturally, the truckers were proud of their Susie. After all, not many outfits, if any, can boast such a well behaved young lady as their mascot.

But there has been one thing neglected in Susie's conversion to the American way of life. She is still minus shoes. The gang didn't notice this defect, as Susie didn't seem to mind the fact that she was still barefoot, and was able to get her exercise despite the presence of many rocks.

However, Susie must have noticed that she wasn't completely American, as recently she appeared at the Post Dispensary for an examination of the feet. 1st Lt. James S. Jessup, MC. after a close examination of the feet, wrote to the MTS headquarters, recommending that Susie be fitted with shoes as quickly as possible.

The lieutenant wrote: "Due to the condition of the feet and the nature of the duties to be performed, it is recommended that Pfc Susie M. T. Ass, U-36458609 be properly fitted with G. I. shoes, since the English-made shoes have no arch support and might cause injury to the feet."

So, Susie is going to get some shoes. They will be good, sturdy, steel shoes, too as befits an up and coming young burro. The MTS gang will supervise the making of the shoes by the blacksmith, to make sure they are suitable for the outfit's popular mascot.

Cpl. Sam Greenberg

For ease of reading, here is a copy of the article.

Susie Needs Pair of Shoes But MTS Gang Won't Depend on Crap Game

Susie, a native of Persia was adopted several months ago by the boys of MTS headquarters, She was then typical of the country — thin and emaciated, and didn't have any shoes.

The MTS gang took good care of Susie. Under the careful eyes of GI dieticians, she has filled out admirably. Her ribs are no longer visible through her skin, and her body is filled out perfectly so that now she is among the finest of her type.

Naturally, the truckers were proud of their Susie. After all, not many outfits, if any, can boast such a well behaved young lady as their mascot.

But there has been one thing neglected in Susie's conversion to the American way of life. She is still minus shoes. The gang didn't notice this defect, as Susie didn't seem to mind the fact she was still barefoot, and was able to get her exercise despite the presence of many rocks.

However, Susie must have noticed that she wasn't completely American, as recently she appeared at the Post Dispensary for an examination of the feet. 1st Lt. James S. Jessup, MC. after a close examination of the feet, wrote to the MTS headquarters recommending that Susie be fitted with shoes as quickly as possible.

The lieutenant wrote: "Due to the condition of the feet and the nature of the duties to be performed, it is recommended that Pfc Susie M.T.Ass. D–36458609 be properly fitted with G.I. shoes, since the English-made shoes have no arch support and might cause injury to the feet."

So, Susie is going to get some shoes. They will be good, sturdy, steel shoes, too as befits an up and coming young burro. The MTS gang will supervise the making of the shoes by the blacksmith. To make sure they are suitable for the outfit's popular mascot.

Cpl. Sam Greenberg

This photo was taken in Kazvin, Iran. Again, during this century, it is called Qazvin. It is located in the Qazvin province. Sam called it a Great Mosque. Its proper name is James Mosque.

Jameh Mosque of Qazvin, and it is one of the oldest Mosques in Iran.[22]

IRAN - 1943 - GREAT MOSQUE - KAZVIN
(3)
PARTS ARE 800 YEARS OLD

"Pvt. Howard Saring Is Champion Sharp-shooter; He Bags Partridge."

This article was published in the United States Army Dispatch. Private Saring discusses the differences between shooting rats on a

Philadelphia dump and shooting gazelle, boar, and rabbit from a truck as an MTS driver.

UNITED STATES ARMY DISPATCH

Pvt. Howard Saring Is Champion Sharpshooter; He Bags Partridge

Shooting rats on a Philadelphia dump is a far cry from shooting gazelle, boar or rabbit on a desert in Iran. But Pvt. Howard W. Saring of the Quaker city went through that transition recently when he bagged a quail and a rabbit which is mighty fine shooting from a GI truck.

Saring, an MTS driver on duty with post utilities as a plumber, was a sharp shooter at the age of 13 when he hunted the rodents with a long range Mossberg. 22. The shooting skill he gained as a boy stood him in good stead on his hunting trip in Persia.

Driving a carryall last February through the mountains from a southern staging area to his destination in the mountains Saring had a rough time, as his vehicle slid around the curves for most of the way.

Saring relates an unusual incident when he was almost killed by a train. ‹I had taken a short cut›, he said ‹and stopped between the ties on the track to pick up a stone when I heard the limited coming. Instead of taking three steps and getting clear of the track I became frightened and found myself in a petrified state. Then a queer thing happened. I thought of the time when I'd almost drowned in the Delaware from a leg cramp, I somehow snapped out of it and hauled myself off the tracks. I was sweating as the train roared by›. Saring is looking forward to retiring to a small farm in Pennsylvania after the war-and of course he'll have a bride with him!

Cpl. Sam Greenberg

Here is a reprint for clarity.

United States Army Dispatch

Pvt Howard Saring Is Champion Sharpshooter; He Bags Partridge

Shooting rats on a Philadelphia dump is a far cry from shooting gazelle, boar or rabbit on a desert in Iran. But Pvt. Howard W. Saring of the Quaker city went through that transition recently when he bagged a quail and a rabbit which is mighty fine shooting from a GI truck.

Saring, an MTS driver on duty with post utilities as a plumber, was a sharp shooter at the age of 13 when he hunted the rodents with a long range Mossberg. 22. The shooting skill he gained as a boy stood him in good stead on his hunting trip in Persia.

Driving a carryall last February through the mountains from a southern staging area to his destination in the mountains Saring had a rough time, as his vehicle slid around the curves most of the way.

Saring relates an unusual incident when he was almost killed by a train. "I had taken a short cut," he said "and stopped between the ties on the track to pick up a stone when I heard the limited coming. Instead of taking three steps and getting clear of the track I became frightened and found myself in a petrified state. Then a queer thing happened. I thought of the time when I'd almost drowned in the Delaware from a leg cramp. I somehow snapped out of it and hauled myself off the tracks. I was sweating as the train roared by". Saring is looking forward to retiring to a small farm in Pennsylvania after the war and of course he'll have a bride with him!

Cpl. Sam Greenberg

On the next page is a photo of a Musallah or ancient site of a citadel at Hamadan. Sam misspelled Musallah as the correct spelling is Musalla.

A musalla is an open space outside a mosque, mainly used for prayer in Islam. A musalla may also refer to a room, structure, or place for conducting canonical prayers and is usually translated as a "prayer hall" smaller than a mosque.[23]

A citadel is the core fortified area of a town or city.[24]

IRAN - 1943 -- MUSALLAH ON ANCIENT SITE
⑤
OF CITADEL AT HAMADAN —

"General Handy Man of Engineers Builds Water Heater That Works."

Sam often wrote about other soldiers and gave us their stories. This article was about Sergeant Lee A. Freeland of Holbrook, Arizona. When Sergeant Freeland was not on his bulldozer working on the roads, he was creating some new device that made a job easier.

General Handy Man of Engineers Builds Water Heater That Works

He's a soft-spoken, modest guy who used to hunt in Texas and Arizona. He drove a truck in the States. Out here in Iran as a member of Company E, 363d Engineers, he has coaxed a bulldozer over many a road job, and guided a caterpall into laying dirt in the right place, with precision.

Builds Heaters

Before the war, he did welding on construction jobs. Today, his inventiveness has him in great demand, building those heaters which keep the water hot for washing mess kits. He has helped on carpentry work, ha can barber and do blacksmithing. Give him a balky cigarette lighter or a bum ice cream freezer and he'll get them working.

He can fashion a swell tempered knife from a good file and he has hit a wild boar at a distance of 750 yards, although he admits his shots were lucky.

He is Sgt. Lee A. Freeland of Holbrook, Arizona. His water heater idea is an adaptation of a similar arrangement on tar tank trucks. Recently the sergeant, noticing that the water for washing mess kits wasn't heating fast enough, conceived his idea and drew a diagram. Official approval being given, he built the apparatus in his spare time.

The device consists of a 12-gallon tank of fuel, an ordinary tire pump and a pipe leading to the brick furnace. Three minutes of work with the pump supplies enough pressure to feed the fuel to keep the fire going for an hour and a half, and the system heats a 20-gallon can of water in 45 minutes.

Shoots Boar

Telling about his boar shooting, Freeland said, we were way up in the mountains when I sighted this hog. I kneeled, and hit him four out of five times. Each time he got up I'd fire another shot. On getting closer to the game animal I saw that both front legs had been shot off, and there was a bullet hole in the hind leg and one in the shoulder.

<The boar somehow managed to hobble along and, with the help of my native guide we tracked and chased it down to the road, where I finished him off with a final close shot.

Cpl. Sam Greenberg

Again, reprinted for clarity.

General Handy Man of Engineers Builds
Water Heater That Works

He's a soft-spoken, modest guy who used to hunt in Texas and Arizona. He drove a truck in the States. Out here in Iran as a member of Company E. 363d Engineers, he has coaxed a bulldozer over many a road job, and guided a carryall into laying dirt in the right place, with precision.

Builds Heaters

Before the war, he did welding on construction jobs. Today, his inventiveness has him in great demand, building those heaters which keep the water hot for washing mess kits. He has helped on carpentry work, he can barber and do blacksmithing. Give him a balky cigarette lighter or a bum ice cream freezer and he'll get them working.

He can fashion a swell tempered knife from a good file and he has a hit a wild boar at a distance of 750 yards, although he admits his shots were lucky.

He is Sgt. Lee A. Freeland of Holbrook, Arizona. His water heater idea is an adaptation of a similar arrangement on tar tank trucks. Recently the sergeant noticing that the water for washing mess kits wasn't heating fast enough, conceived his idea and drew a diagram. Official approval being given he built the apparatus in his spare time.

The device consists of a 12-gallon tank of fuel, an ordinary tire pump and a pipe leading to the brick furnace. Three minutes of work with the pump supplies enough pressure to feed the fuel to keep the fire going for an hour and a half, and the system heats a 20-gallon can of water in 45 minutes.

Shoots Boar

Telling about his boar shooting, Freeland said, we were way up in the mountains when I sighted this hog. I kneeled, and hit him four out of five times. Each time he got up I'd fire another shot. On getting closer to the game animal I saw that both front legs had been shot off, and there was a bullet hole in the hind leg and one in the shoulder.

The boar somehow managed to hobble along and, with the help of my native guide we tracked and chased it down the road, where I finished him off with a final close shot.

Cpl. Sam Greenberg

Sam went to the city of Dizful (Dezful), Iran. In the first photo Sam states that Dizful is the oldest and hottest city in the world. He also states that it is believed to be the biblical "City of Rats." While it is old, it is not the oldest city in the world. As far as it being the "biblical City of Rats," I cannot find any reference to it in the Old or New Testaments. I wouldn't doubt that the city has had a rat problem for quite some time, though. The second photo shows why Sam's comment would be "God Bless America".

25) CITY OF DIZFUL, SOMETIMES TERMED OLDEST & HOTTEST CITY IN WORLD - BELIEVED TO BE BIBLICAL "CITY OF RATS" - INHABITANTS LIVE IN UNDERGROUND LABYRINTH OF CHAMBERS & TUNNELS THROUGHOUT LONG, HOT SUMMERS!

IRAN - 1943

26) STREET SCENE. DIZFUL - SEE #25 CAPTION

IRAN - 1943

LOOK AT THIS SCENE & GOD BLESS AMERICA!!!

The following is a scanned letter from the managing Editor, Marion White, of the magazine called "The Woman With Woman's Digest." The letter was dated December 16, 1943. They were going to publish an article that Sam wrote titled "Five Don'ts For The Girl Back Home." It was published in the April 1944 edition of the magazine.

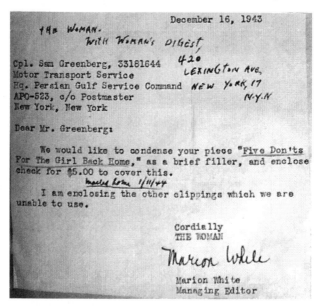

This article is about Private Charles G. Basales of Paterson, New Jersey. On his 30 day furlough, he visited relatives that he had never seen in Aleppo, Syria. He made a stop in Damascus, Syria; took a tour of Tel-Aviv in Palestine; and visited the pyramids in Egypt. It was published on Dec. 13, 1943.

For ease of reading, here is a copy of the article.

12/13/43

GI Visits Egypt, Syrian Relatives On 30-day Leave

He's got relatives in Rome, Cairo, South America, Africa, Australia and Syria. Syria is close to Iran, but Pvt. Charles G. Basales, of Paterson, N.J., who failed to even get a three-day pass in the States before going overseas, figured he might have better luck over here. He did.

He's just back from a 30-day furlough. His aunts and uncles in Aleppo, Syria, which is approximately 2000 miles from Iran, had never seen Charles but they recognized him immediately. His mother had sent his picture to them seven years go.

Highlights of his trip were a stop in Damascus, capital of Syria, where the famous Damascus swords are wrought by hand; a tour of Tel-Aviv in Palestine and a visit to one of the fabulous pyramids of Egypt.

"With a war going on," short, stocky Basales, of Co. B, 80th Engineer Battalion, said with a grin, "I was lucky to be able to take such a fascinating trip. I travelled by train, truck and car. No difficulties. My knowledge of Arabic made things easy for me as this lingo is the native tongue in Syria.

"In the center of Aleppo there is an ancient castle over 5000 years old. In it kings used to live in regal splendor. Now the castle is empty and is pointed out to all sightseers. I saw the cavernous dungeons underground and the slits in the walls of the castle from which archer warriors used to shoot their arrows at any invaders.

"Then"

Sam sent this home on December 18, 1943. It centered on his observations and experiences of a year earlier, when first arriving in Iran.

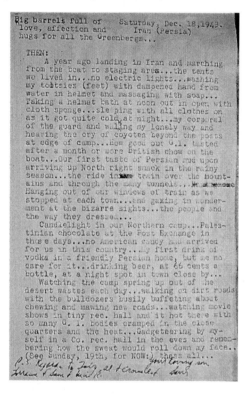

I have retyped for clarity.

Saturday, Dec. 18, 1943
Iran (Persia)
Big barrels full of love, affection and hugs for all the Greenbergs...

THEN:

    A year ago landing in Iran and marching from the boat to staging area... the tents we lived

in... no electric lights... washing my tootsies
(feet) with dampened hand from water in helmet
and massaging with soap... Taking a helmet bath
at noon out in open with cloth sponge... sleeping with all clothes on as it got quite cold at
night... my corporal of the guard and walking my
lonely way and hearing the cry of coyotes beyond
the posts at edge of camp... How good our G.I.
tasted after a month or more British chow on the
boat... Our first taste of Persian mud upon arriving up North right smack in the rainy season...
the ride in train over the mountains and through
the many tunnels... Hanging out of our windows of
train as we stopped at each town... and gazing in
wonderment at the bizarre sights... the people
and the way they dressed...

Candlelight in our Northern camp... Palestinian
chocolate at the Post Exchange in those days...
no American candy had arrived for us in this
country... My first drink of vodka in a friendly
Persian home, but me no care for it... drinking
beer, at 66 cents a bottle, at a night spot in
town close by...

Watching the camp spring up out of the desert
wastes each day... walking on dirt roads with
the bulldozers busily buffeting about chewing
and mawing new roads... watching movie shows in
tiny rec. hall in the eves and remembering how
the sweat would roll down my face... (See Sunday,
19th, for NOW:) thass all...

                                        Your loving son
                                        Sam

"Now"

A second letter that Sam sent home the next day, December 19, 1943. It was a summary of all of the changes that a year can make. Probably one big highlight of the year for Sam was receiving a publicity photo of Rita Hayworth, who was a famous American actress and dancer.

Again, reprinted for clarity.

Sunday, Dec. 19, 1943.
Iran (Persia).

The sweetest of love and kisses for all the Greenbergs...

NOW:

Our barracks, with their nudes and pinups,
aren't bad at all... Just got my photo from Rita
Hayworth, but it just a publicity shot from the
studio... lovely, though... Lights are electric...
Our shower room just had a stove installed and
we have hot water most of the time... Chow is
great with fresh meats and butter... When it
rains out here, things not so bad, as roads are
o.k. and there are plenty of gravel paths that
soak in the rain, therefore no mud... Plenty of
American candy at the PX at times: on hand now
are Hershey's tropical chocolate blocks; toot-
sie rools, Necco wafers, and life savers... Beer
at the PX in cans sells for 2 rials, 6 cents...
Starting tomorrow our ration for the next ten
days will be increased to 11 cans... We'll have
a nice Christmas and New Year... Our new rec hall
is a spacious affair with large reading room, soft
chairs; large writing room, library... and a large
play room with tables (this converted into dance
floor on Saturday nights) and plenty of ping pong
tables... And the theater seats about 700 G.I.'s
at one sitting... nice stage for our own G.I. shows
and visiting USO shows... Acoustics for our sound
movies are O.K.... Not a bad set-up at all... We
have small portable stoves for our barracks... not
like those wood burning large ones last winter...
Susie has quite a large corral on ground adjacent
to our barracks... Will take a pic of with her one
of these days... Close to our area the ASF band
plays many times during the day in their practice
sessions and we pass them on our way back from

work at noon chow... Time is now 7:55 p.m. and
time for some literati... keep well all.

> Your loving son
>
> Sam

She came to popularity in the 1940's and was one of that
era's top stars. The Press coined the term "Love Goddess"
to describe her. She was the top pin-up girl for GIs during
World War II.[25]

*A publicity photo from the film "Down to Earth," this is typical
of the many publicity photos sent out of Rita Hayworth.*[26]

This was a group photo of the soldiers involved in Headquarters Motor Transport Service. There are 67 soldiers in this photo and you can find Sam on the top row, all the way to the left. The Zagros Mountains are in the background.

Beyond the vast expanse of desert dunes were the Zagros Mountains with peaks that rose more than 16,000 feet. Temperatures there dropped to 25 degrees below zero with year round snow cover on the mountaintops.[27]

Chapter Six

1944

THE LETTER SCANNED here seems to be a partial letter showing only the end of Sam's thoughts. He wrote about how hobbies can keep one in good health. He made note of this to his Pop.

```
    Follows a pertinent quote re hobbies...
"And science of preventive medicine agrees.
(Pop take note...) It points out, for exam-
ple, that you can ride a hobby to health...
A hobby is fine protection against old fogy-
ism.  It adds zest to living, may offer scope
for mild exercise and nearly always is a
first rate antidote to worry, strain and
anxiety.  It really doesn't matter what you
do--wood carving, fishing, religion, garden-
ing, collecting stamps, books, or butterfly
wings.  Or just twiddling your toes in the
sun.  A hobby gives you a chance to escape,
to find yourself again--your "youth of mind."
    "What nonsense!"  snort the skeptics.
"Where would the world be if we wasted time
by twiddling our toes in the sun?"
    Probably further ahead and a lot happier,
reply the philosophers.
    Thass all and digest the above..keep well
```

P.S. Regards to Joly, al &
Lorraine & Cromwell &
Sam & Mun K.

your loving son
Sam

The following is a partial copy of Sam's letter.

1944 Persia

Follows a pertinent quote re hobbies ... "And science of preventive medicine agrees. (Pop take note...) It points out, for example, that you can ride a hobby to health ... A hobby is fine protection against old fogyism. It adds zest to living, may offer scope for mild exercise and nearly always is a first rate antidote to worry, strain and anxiety. It really doesn't matter what you do—wood carving, fishing, religion, gardening, collecting stamps, books, or butterfly wings. Or just twiddling your toes in the sun. A hobby gives you a chance to escape, to find yourself again—your "youth of mind."

"What nonsense!" snort the skeptics. "Where would the world be if we wasted time by twiddling our toes in the sun?"

Probably further ahead and a lot happier, reply the philosophers.

Thass all and digest the above . . keep well

Your loving son
Sam

Sam came up with an idea for a cartoon. He wrote the cartoon and came up with the visual ideas. An artist illustrated the cartoon. It was humorous and was subsequently published in the Army Laughs section in January 1944.

This article's title is "On Being Considerate".
He sums it up by observing the rights and
feelings of others, according to Webster.

The following is a copy of Sam's publication.

On Being Considerate

Show me a guy who is considerate — and you've shown me a right
guy: a person with fine character!

Being a soldier throws you in with
fellows from all walks of life, from all
strata of society!

Some are rough, unpolished, but
with hearts of gold!

On Being Considerate

SHOW me a guy who is considerate—
and you've shown me a right guy: a
person with a fine character!

Being a soldier throws you in with fellows from all walks of life, from all strata
of society!

Some are rough, unpolished, but with
hearts of gold!

Others are smooth, clean outwardly,
but selfish and inconsiderate to the core!
And still others are uncouth, rottenly
aggressive, and the Army won't change
them into better beings because their inherent make-up shuns betterment: their
ego and creed are stilted into channels of
so-called toughness! Hurry for me and to
hell with the other guy!

Being considerate is being observant of
the rights and feelings of others, according to Webster. And how very true this
is, can be applied to everyday Army life!

In the chow line, don't bust in ahead
of others!

In the barracks, don't hog too much
space and have your barracks bags floating all over the place!

After sweeping around your cot, help
in police-up of the center aisle—do your
part—think of the other guy!

In the recreation hall, during a movie
show, if up front don't sit on a table, thus
blocking the view of so many other soldiers behind you!

On a hike don't be slow to help the
other chap adjust his pack strap. A compliment, now and then, will help also!

The line on practical jokes can be
drawn thus:—would you like the same
stunt pulled on you? If not, don't you
pull it on the other guy!

In final analysis: don't beef too much—
do your part—be considerate.

—*Corporal Sam Greenberg, in the Middle East*

Others are smooth, clean outwardly, but selfish and inconsiderate to the core!

And still others are uncouth, rottenly aggressive, and the Army won't change them into better beings because their inherent make-up shuns betterment: their ego and creed are stilted into channels of so-called toughness! Hurray for me and to hell with the other guy!

Being considerate is being observant of the rights and feelings of others, according to Webster. And how very true this is, can be applied to everyday Army life!

In the chow line, don't bust in ahead of others!

In the barracks, don't hog too much space and have your barracks bags floating all over the place!

After sweeping around your cot, help in police-up of the center aisle—do your part—think of the other guy!

In the recreation hall, during a movie show, if up front don't sit on a table, thus blocking the view of so many other soldiers behind you!

On a hike don't be slow to help the other chap adjust his pack strap. A compliment, now and then, will help also!

The line on practical jokes can be drawn thus:—would you like the same stunt pulled on you? If not, don't you pull it on the other guy!

In final analysis: don't beef too much—do your part—be considerate.

—*Corporal Sam Greenberg, in the Middle East*

A published note from "The Steno" in Army Laughs magazine about some of the boys she hears from "all the way over in Persia," two being Corporal Sam Greenberg and Private Lew Levy.

Here is a retype from the Steno in Army Laughs.

Army Laughs' Steno says "Hello"

Hello Boys:

Just when I was trying to get Bobby Bleier out of my hair, I received a letter from him telling me that he has just been awarded a metal for sharpshooting. Congrats to you, Bobby!

Cpl. Sam Greenberg and Pvt. Lew Levy, old friends of ours, have not lost their Yankee sense of humor.

Although they're now way over in Persia the jokes they send in are a scream to me.

Among the servicemen's snapshots submitted today for "About Faces" Dave Kohnhorst, Wm. Beau. Gen. Hosp., El Paso, Texas, is my choice. Girls, is he handsome! His caricature will probably appear in the next issue of Army Laughs. So much for the males …

Did you guys ever hear the one about the rookie who fought the owl with a barn shovel and couldn't see the sun for feathers? Am I good!

Yours till the Axis is Axed!

THE STENO

Here is a scan of Sam's published article printed in the magazine called "The Woman With Woman's Digest" in the April 1944 edition. The article's title is "Five Don'ts for the Girl Back Home". This is a follow-up relating to the letter that Sam received from the magazine's managing editor, Marion White, the previous year on December 16, 1943.

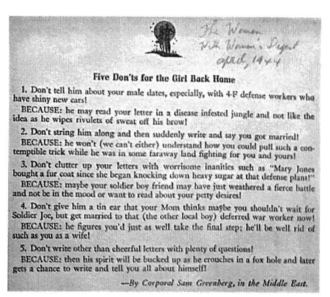

Five Don'ts for the Girl Back Home

1. Don't tell him about your male dates, especially, with 4-F defense workers who have shiny new cars!
BECAUSE: he may read your letter in a disease infested jungle and not like the idea as he wipes rivulets of sweat off his brow!

2. Don't string him along and then suddenly write and say you got married!
BECAUSE: he won't (we can't either) understand how you could pull such a contemptible trick while he was in some faraway land fighting for you and yours!

3. Don't clutter up your letters with worrisome inanities such as "Mary Jones bought a fur coat since she began knocking down heavy sugar at that defense plant!"
BECAUSE: maybe your soldier boy friend may have just weathered a fierce battle and not be in the mood or want to read about your petty desires!

4. Don't give him a tin ear that your Mom thinks maybe you shouldn't wait for Soldier Joe, but get married to that (the other local boy) deferred war worker now!
BECAUSE: he figures you'd just as well take the final step; he'll be well rid of such as you as a wife!

5. Don't write other than cheerful letters with plenty of questions!
BECAUSE: then his spirit will be bucked up as he crouches in a fox hole and later gets a chance to write and tell you all about himself!

—By Corporal Sam Greenberg, in the Middle East.

For ease of reading, here is a copy of the article.

The Woman With Woman's Digest
April, 1944

Five Don'ts for the Girl Back Home

1. Don't tell him about your male dates, especially, with 4-F defense workers who have shiny new cars!

BECAUSE: he may read your letter in a disease infested jungle and not like the idea as he wipes rivulets of sweat off his brow!

2. Don't string him along and then suddenly write and say you got married!

BECAUSE: he won't (we can't either) understand how you could pull such a contemptible trick while he was in some faraway land fighting for you and yours!

3. Don't clutter up your letters with worrisome inanities such as "Mary Jones bought a fur coat since she began knocking down heavy sugar at that defense plant!"

BECAUSE: maybe your soldier boy friend may have just weathered a fierce battle and not be in the mood or want to read about your petty desires!

4. Don't give him a tin ear that your Mom thinks maybe you shouldn't wait for Soldier Joe, but get married to that (the other local boy) deferred war worker now!

BECAUSE: he figures you'd just as well take the final step; he'll be well rid of such as you as a wife!

5. Don't write other than cheerful letters with plenty of questions!

BECAUSE: then his spirit will be bucked up as he crouches in a fox hole and later gets a chance to write and tell you all about himself!

—By Corporal Sam Greenberg, in the Middle East

The following is the beginning of a letter Sam sent home. In the first part, Sam recounted some wonderful advice that his Chief of Staff, General George C. Marshall, gave to his wife. The next part was a quote from Lena Horne, singing screen star.

Here is a reprint for clarity.

> Monday, April 3, 1944.
> Iran (Persia).

Straight doses of hugs, kisses and etc., for Mom, Pop, Gilda and Herman ...

Wonderful advice given to his wife by General George C. Marshall, our Chief of Staff:

"Whenever I worry about something that has happened, he tells me, 'You're wasting your time.

When a thing is done, it's done. You can't change
it. Even God can't change it, so why worry?'"

   And Lena Horne, the sepia singing screen star,
now, handles the Hollywood wolf nicely:

   "She receiveds their attentions graciously and
then adds kindly, 'Come up to the house and meet
the children and my mother!'"

Lena Horne was an American singer, actress, dancer, and civil rights
activist. As an actress throughout her life, she performed on stage,
television, and in movies. The letter that dad sent home was dated
April 03, 1944.

Lena, in the opinion of many, Lena's best movies were made
in 1943, notably "Stormy Weather" and "Cabin in the Sky."[1]

Both sides of her family were a mixture of African-American,
Native American, and European American descent and
belonged to the upper stratum of middle-class, well-educated
people.[2]

This photo is Lena Horne
in "Till the Clouds Roll By"
(1946). It is a Studio publicity still.

Taken in April 1944, this is an interior view of the Motor Transport Service headquarters.

Sam is in this photo at Motor Transport Service headquarters before mess call, dinner.

In this photo, you can see the two minarets or towers where the call to prayer is announced in this mosque.

This photo shows a street scene in Teheran, the capital of Iran.

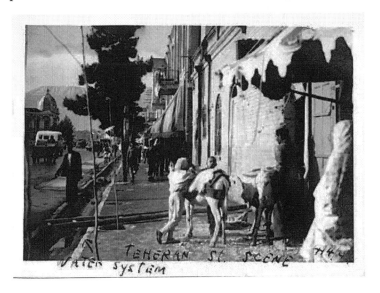

All of these photos taken in April 1944 show different aspects found in Iran during WWII.

This photo shows the table set for Seder, April 7th, 1944.

The Passover Seder is a Jewish ritual feast that marks the beginning of the Jewish holiday of Passover. It is observed every year on the 15th day of Nisan in the Hebrew calendar. This corresponds to late March or early April in the Western calendar.

> Passover in the Jewish faith is a holiday where Jewish people remember their liberation by God from slavery in Egypt through the leadership of Moses. It is the story of the Exodus as described in the Old Testament.[3]

This scan is a second publishing of the same article that was first published in April of the same year, in "The Woman with Woman's Digest." This time, it was in an Army publication keeping the same title, "Five Don'ts for the Girl Back Home." It was published in May 1944.

Five Don'ts for the Girl Back Home

1. Don't tell him about your male dates, especially, with 4-F defense workers who have shiny new cars!

BECAUSE: he may read your letter in a disease infested jungle and not like the idea as he wipes rivulets of sweat off his brow!

2. Don't string him along and then suddenly write and say you got married!

BECAUSE: he won't (we can't either) understand how you could pull such a contemptible trick while he was in some faraway land fighting for you and yours!

3. Don't clutter up your letters with worrisome inanities such as "Mary Jones bought a fur coat since she began knocking down heavy sugar at that defense plant!"

BECAUSE: maybe your soldier boy friend may have just weathered a fierce battle and not be in the mood or want to read about your petty desires!

4. Don't give him a tin ear that your Mom thinks maybe you shouldn't wait for Soldier Joe, but get married to that (the other local boy) deferred war worker now!

BECAUSE: he figures you'd just as well take the final step; he'll be well rid of such as you as a wife!

5. Don't write other than cheerful letters with plenty of questions!

BECAUSE: then his spirit will be bucked up as he crouches in a fox hole and later gets a chance to write and tell you all about himself!

—*By Corporal Sam Greenberg, in the Middle East.*

Here we find a photo of the Persian Gulf Command Insignia at the base of the flagpole at the entrance to the M.T.S. headquarters.

Here, side by side, is a scan of Sam's Persian Gulf Command Insignia. To the right of Sam's Insignia is a cleaner version found on the Persian Gulf Command Veterans Organization website.

In 1943, this new insignia was developed for the soldiers of The Pacific Gulf Command. They designed a shield of vivid green ornamented with a crimson saber, outlined in white. Above and to the right of the saber is a white seven-pointed star. The three colors, crimson, green, and white appear in the flags of Iraq and Iran. The star is on the flag of Iraq. For the U.S. the saber signifies that this is a combat outfit, while in the Islamic world, the saber was always the sign of the ruling class.

Crimson, white and green have significance in the Moslem world. Green is not only the family color of Mohammed, but also signified the fertility once current in Iraq, particularly in the area where the Garden of Eden is reputed to have been. When Mohammed died, there was a schism among his followers and an offshoot decided to adopt white as its official emblem, a symbol of purity. There was a later revolt within the Moslem ranks. It created the formation of the Alhambrian Caliphate which adopted crimson as its color as a symbol of Islam's conquests and the blood that was shed.[4]

In the photo, the arrow at the bottom points to Sam. This is one good way to cool off.

In this letter dated April 6, 1944, Sam states that regarding success, the only given is the opportunity for it. A successful outcome is dependent on many things, among them hard work, perseverance, and one's own character.

```
Short, choppy        Thursday, April 6, 1944.
hugs and jolting       Iran (Persia).
kisses for Mom, Pop,
Gilda and Herman.....

     Sittin! and wishin'
     Won't change your fate.
     The Lord provides the fishin',
     But you have to dig the bait!
(Culled from some misc. source)....Which
brings me to the following bit on OPPORTUNITY
to wit:
     It is foolish to say that the world owes
any one a living. Rather should we advocate
realization of the fact that there is offered
only opportunity for success, and even this
is dependent on one's character, persever-
ance, and hard work....
```

With a couple of scanned words that are hard to read, you can read the following.

Thursday, April 6, 1944.
Iran (Persia).

Short, choppy hugs and jolting kisses for Mom, Pop, Gilda and Herman... ...

Sittin' and wishin'
Won't change your fate.
The Lord provides the fishin;,
But you have to dig the bait!

(Culled from some misc. source)... Which brings to me to the following bit on OPPORTUNITY to wit:

It is foolish to say that the world owes any one a living. Rather should we advocate realization of

```
the fact that there is offered only opportunity
for success, and even this is dependent on one's
character, perseverance, and hard work...
```

Another V-Mail sent home to Mom for Mother's Day on May 1, 1944.
It looks like he wanted to make sure it got there on time!

Sam on guard in Iran.

The following scan is a published article titled "Rookie Raves" by
Corporals Sam Greenberg and Lew Levy, "Writing From Somewhere
in Persia." From the words in the article, I think that they were in
Tehran, Iran. In addition, it appears Private Levy got promoted? It
came out in June of 1944. Although the photo is not the best, Sam is
on the lower left. In the middle is Staff Sergeant Stephen W. Bumball,
with John J. Pisaturo on the right. They tell us about the natives, places
to eat, the local rodeo, and of course, the girls.

Another retype for clarity.

Rookie Raves

By CORPORALS SAM GREENBERG and LEW LEVY

Writing From Somewhere in Persia

If you think Florida is home of the palms, soldier, you should be here… Everybody has their hand out! The first words that greet you are: "Buchshees, Johnnie!" That's native for "Buddy, can you spare a dime!"… The next words are also "Bucksheesh, Johnnie, Bucksheesh"… Boy, does basic training come in handy here… Remember, back at camp during our early training, the Sergeant telling us to keep our hands out of our pockets while policing the area… Sure, but we knew better and kept them in… When they ask for Bucksheesh and you shell out they tell you where to go… And if you don't shell out, well, they tell you where to go anyway!…

Like all soldiers, we too, are always hungry… Remember the signs back home, "Keep off the Grass"… Here they read, "Don't eat the grass"… This is a paradise for any Democrat… There are so many donkeys here, you can pick your version of your favorite politician… Horses are expensive… Last Sunday cost me $10.00… I've discovered it's wrong to bet on horses, the way I do! And they even have rodeos here … It seems slinging the bull is universal. Could it be that the local cowboy who broke his neck at the rodeo got himself a bum steer?… Now let's come to the city of— … It's the Gharry's graveyard (Gharry: no relation to Cooper) a horse-drawn vehicle somewhat like a carriage… When you ride in one you're not sure whether the driver is on the seat or if he has exchanged places with the horse… The driver sits above you; the horse sits on you … Anyway, the part of him that chases flies away, and believe he doesn't take a back seat for any one…

The city, where it's not the heat, it's the humanity… And, Boy, there's plenty of hustle and bustle … Plenty more hustle than bustle… This city is a Soldier's town… With all the uniforms everywhere, Errol Flynn would certainly feel at home… As usual, the military objective is girls… And after that, more girls… There are many cabarets and restaurants here… We went to the finest restaurant the other night and filled ourselves full of costly groceries to the brim… In the process we managed to empty our pockets of paper money which looks like second-hand stock certificates so familiar back in 1929... You have to buy a large-sized wallet to keep them in, but after you buy the wallet you don't have any left to put in...

They have a great chef here... He's been cooking for 20 years... He ought to be done by now... But, no kidding, Bud, this place is really high class... They make gravy in all colors to match any uniform... They serve onions which don't leave any after breath... But, when they give you the bill it takes your breath away... Even here they know all about western sandwiches... You know the kind: two hunks of bread with wide open spaces between...

But why should I keep you in suspense... You want to know about the girls... What soldier doesn't? Even I still want to know about them... But seriously, Bud, we had a couple of dishes (dames, I mean, even tho' they were a little cracked)... We took them — (excuse me — they took us) — The dish I had spoke seven different languages... And knew how to say "No" in every one... She used to be a chorus girl and got her education by stages... Bill got himself a college girl... She got her education by degrees... She knew her degrees... She was a cold number but she certainly made it hot for him... Her name was Rosy... I wondered why Bill kept his arm around her all night long... He told me he was playing a new game called "Wing Around Rosy"... The dame I had was a corker... Always mumbling to herself... Finally I said: "Honey, if you don't feel good why don't you go home to Mutter"... Bill almost got us in dutch... He asked his dish where she lived... Wouldn't it have been funny if she'd said China... Although it would have been a new slant… Any way he's funny that way, he always wants to know where they live so he'll know just how far he can go with the girl… We leave and hail a gharry… With the prices they charge you are justified in saying, "Home, Jesse James"… Well, we finally ditch the dishes and retreat to our home grounds for an early bedcheck and find the top-kick all in because he went all out for his Persian Versian… Any way, like the new bridegroom said: "I never knew you could have so much fun without laughing!"

Here is the photo that was cropped and used in the "Rookie Raves" article.

The title above the articles photo is "Our Author in Iran". Below the photo it says: Left, in the picture, is Corporal Sam Greenberg, on duty somewhere in Iran or Persia. With him are Staff Sergeant Stephen W. Bumball and Sergeant John J. Pisaturo. Behind the three is their Iranian rickshaw boy and rickshaw.

The following is a short poem co-authored by Corporal Sam Greenberg and Private Lew Levy, published in July 1944, in which they
expressed a desire for the lease-lend of actress Myrna Loy.

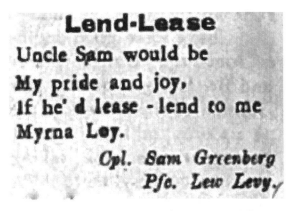

Lend-Lease
Uncle Sam would be
My pride and joy,
If he' d lease - lend to me
Myrna Loy.
                    Cpl. Sam Greenberg
                        Pfc. Lew Levy.

Myrna Loy was an American film, television and stage actress.
Trained as a dancer, Loy devoted herself entirely to an acting
career following a few minor roles in silent films. Although

Loy never received a nomination for a competitive Academy Award, in March 1991, she was presented with an honorary Academy Award in recognition of her life's work both onscreen and off.[5]

At the time of this poem's publication in July of 1944, Myrna Loy's last movie was "Shadow of the Thin Man".

She made another film in 1945 before she left Hollywood for New York, where she volunteered with the Red Cross.[6]

This was another short poem co-authored by Corporal Sam Greenberg and Private Lew Levy. It is a humorous poem titled "Utopia" and was published in July 1944.

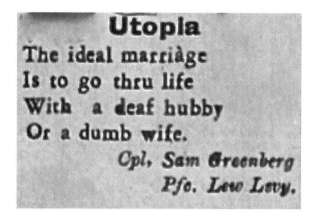

Utopia
The ideal marriage
Is to go thru life
With a deaf hubby
Or a dumb wife.
              Cpl. Sam Greenberg
              Pfc. Lew Levy.

Farm scene in Iran on July 1944.

Here, Sam (on the right) is in Tehran, looking up at a poster of Ken Maynard starring in the singing cowboy movie, Heroes of the Range.

The movie came out in 1936.

A cropped screenshot of Ken Maynard in "In Old Santa Fe" (1934).

The photographer is David Howard.

He first appeared in silent motion pictures in 1923 as a stuntman or supporting actor. In 1924 he began working in western features, where his horsemanship and rugged good looks made him a cowboy star. Maynard's silent features showcased his daredevil riding, photographed fairly close so audiences could see that Maynard was doing his stunts with his white stallion "Tarzan." His reckless screen personality spilled over into his private life, with alcoholism and high living resulting in production delays and temper tantrums on the set. These actions made Maynard a problem employee.[7]

Here this scanned article was titled "Army Glossary" and was published in August 1944. It is full of humor and Sam includes apologies to Army glossaries printed before.

Here is a reprint for clarity.

ARMY GLOSSARY!

(With apologies to Army glossaries printed before…)

SABOTAGE: Soldier stricken with "German" measles!

ACTING GADGET: Acting non-commissioned officers, without pay, who ACT!

STRIPE CRACY: Disliked non-com!

PFC: Pretty fast company!

BRUSH-OFF: When she stops writing "Dearest!"

FURLOUGH: What all soldiers want and a few get!

JEEP: Car in a capsule!

A GLORIFIED GOLD-BRICK: There ain't no such animal!

COLONEL'S ORDERLY: A gold-brick with stripes!

ARMY GLOSSARY!
(With apologies to Army glossaries printed before . . .)
SABOTAGE: Soldier stricken with "German" measles!
ACTING GADGET: Acting non-commissioned officers, without pay, who ACT!
STRIPE CRAZY: Disliked non-com!
PFC: Pretty fast company!
BRUSH-OFF: When she stops writing "Dearest!"
FURLOUGH: What all soldiers want and a few get!
JEEP: Car in a capsule!
A GLORIFIED GOLD-BRICK: There ain't no such animal!
COLONEL'S ORDERLY: A gold-brick with stripes!
CHOW HOUND: He lives to eat!
RUMOR: Method of circulating news of tomorrow—TODAY!
SICK CALL: Gold bricker's virus!
G. I.: Good intentions!
BLIND DATE: A date you hope you never made—but HOPE!
N. C. O.: No comfort allowed!
M. P.: Mis-print or Mis-placed!
SECONDS (on chow): Chow-hound's return trip!
CLASS "A" PASS: Pretty, precious piece of paper!
GAS: Loquaciousness running wild!
HIKE: Something you do with your feet which your mind don't wanna, but your brain registers!
TOP KICK: A guy whose "Kick" registers!
INSUBORDINATION: Saying "No" when you're supposed to say "Yes!"
CHISELER: Tool-less wonder who cuts into everyone!
REVEILLE: The time you get to hate a whistle!
INSURANCE: Protection you should have which you hope you WON'T need!
SHARPSHOOTER: A guy who aims at the bull's-eye and hits what he aims at!
HUMOR: A column which editors swap from each other!
BARRACKS: A place where inspections take place on Saturday mornings!
CAMOUFLAGE: Making yourself into something so that someone else will think you are that something!
CHAPLAIN: Your war-mother, etc., rolled into one!
The Army's perfect listener!
HALT

CHOW HOUND: He lives to eat!

RUMOR: Method of circulating news of tomorrow—TODAY!

SICK CALL: Gold bricker's virus!

G.I: Good intentions!

BLIND DATE: A date you hope you never made—but HOPE!

N.C.O.: No comfort allowed!

M.P.: Mis-print or Mis-placed!

SECONDS (on chow): Chow-hound's return trip!

Class "A" PASS: Pretty, precious piece of paper!

GAS: Loquaciousness running wild!

HIKE: Something you do with your feet which your mind don't wanna, but your brain registers!

TOP KICK: A guy whose "Kick" registers!

INSUBORDINATION: Saying "No" when you're supposed to say "Yes!"

CHISELER: Tool-less wonder who cuts into everyone!

REVEILLE: The time you get to hate a whistle!

INSURANCE: Protection you should have which you hope you WONT' need!

SHARPSHOOTER: A guy who aims at the bull's-eye and hits what he aims at!

HUMOR: A column which editors swap from each other!

BARRACKS: A place where inspections take place on Saturday mornings!

CAMOUFLAGE: Making yourself into something so that someone else will think you are that something!

CHAPLAIN: Your war-mother, etc., rolled into one! The Army's perfect listener!

HALT

This is the Motor Transport Service route, view to the south.

IRAN - 1944 - M.T.S. Route. South

M.P. NATIVE

This article's title is "Advice to the Girls" and was published September 9, 1944. This was Sam's advice to the girls back home. Who knows how many actually got to read it?

For ease of reading, here is another retype.

Advice to the Girls

AFTER THE WAR IS OVER, GIRLS, DON'T—

....ask your boy friend (just back from overseas) how many Japs he killed! (He'll wanna sit and make love to you—not talk!)

....ask your boy friend did he date up gals in lands (he's lucky if there were any around) where he served overseas in the Armed Forces! If he likes you a lot, he'll fib to you; if you don't rate now, he'll go ahead and proceed to hurt your feelings!

....suggest getting married soon, as possibly he has been mulling over the idea many times while soldiering! Besides, he's ripe for the plucking, but don't scare him away! Put the words in his mouth—you figure it out!

....ask him (when you go on your first swimming date) what that tatooed hula dancer on his right forearm is

Sept.

Advice to the Girls

AFTER THE WAR IS OVER, GIRLS, DON'T—

. . . ask your boy friend (just back from overseas) how many Japs he killed! (He'll wanna sit and make love to you —not talk!)

. . . ask your boy friend did he date up gals in lands (he's lucky if there were any around) where he served overseas in the Armed Forces! If he likes you a lot, he'll fib to you; if you don't rate now, he'll go ahead and proceed to hurt your feelings!

. . . . suggest getting married soon, as possibly he has been mulling over the idea many times while soldiering! Besides, he's ripe for the plucking, but don't scare him away! Put the words in his mouth—you figure it out!

. . . . ask him (when you go on your first swimming date) what that tatooed hula dancer on his right forearm is doing. He might tell you the brutal truth and leave you in tears! Let him get around to the story that a bunch of boys were whooping it up and dared him—so he had his skin darned a bit!

. . . . drag him before a group of friends and relatives and expect him to recount his fighting escapades! The only heroes that talk a lot, are manufactured in Hollywood! Besides, it puts him in the limelight, which might be embarrassing; and it might put it out with him!

. . . . keep referring back to the war, or how the civilian population had it tough with rationing, no cars, etc., or soon you'll find it tougher without a boy friend!

. . . . in other words stick your chin out —let him throw the verbal punches!

—*Corporal Sam Greenberg, Somewhere in the Middle East.*

HALT

fib to you; if you don't rate now, he'll go ahead and proceed to hurt your feelings!

....suggest getting married soon, as possibly he has been mulling over the idea many times while soldiering! Besides, he's ripe for the plucking, but don't scare him away! Put the words in his mouth—you figure it out!

....ask him (when you go on your first swimming date) what that tatooed hula dancer on his right forearm is doing. He might tell you the brutal truth and leave you in tears! Let him get around to the story that a bunch of boys were whooping it up and dared him — so he had his skin darned a bit!

....drag him before a group of friends and relatives and expect him to recount his fighting escapades! The only heroes that talk a lot, are manufactured in Hollywood! Besides, it puts him in the limelight, which might be embarrassing; and it might put you out with him!

....keep referring back to the war, or how the civilian population had it tough with rationing, no cars, etc., or soon you'll find it tougher without a boy friend!

....In other words stick your chin out — let him throw the verbal punches!

—*Corporal Sam Greenberg, Somewhere in the Middle East.*

HALT

Two photos of Sam in Hamadan, Iran, on the Jewish holiday Yom Kippur. It was September 29, 1944. This was the last year Sam was in camp and attended the Yom Kippur service.

We find the following article printed in the G.I. Joe & Jane column in the Army publication The Review, Third U.S. Civil Service Region, September 1944, Volume 1, No. 3. It was an article talking of a letter written to, I assume, the Public Ledger, the first newspaper that Sam worked at in Philadelphia, Pennsylvania.

The article presents a letter Sam wrote to The Review writing of some of his recent experiences. He mentions where he was when President Franklin D. Roosevelt visited the troops on the post and Sam was only 10 feet away. He talked about the USO entertainment show that was held where he saw Joe E. Brown, Fredric March, Andre Kostelanetz and Lily Pons.

SAMUAL GREENBURG — Sam is still
stationed in Iran, and wrote us a long
letter, in which he asked to be remembered to various members of the office. Unfortunately, we haven't the space to
print the entire letter, but here are
some of the high points. Sam won't
mind our Philadelphia summers when he
comes back, for the temperature in Iran
hits 126 degrees in the shade. Quote -
Even the camels are taking salt tablets-
unquote. When the President visited
Iran last December to review the troops
on the post, Sam was 10 feet away in a
front rank as he passed by in a jeep.
Sam was also heckled by Joe E. Brown and
saw Frederic March, Andre Kostelanotz
and Lily Pons. Thanks for such an interesting letter Sam, and don't wait so long
before we hear from you again.
    (From G.I. Joe & Jane
        column in THE REVIEW...
        Third U.S. Civil Service
        Region, Sept. 1944,
            Vol. 1, No. 3.)

The following is a copy of that article.

SAMUAL GREENBURG -- Sam is still stationed
in Iran, and wrote us a long letter, in which
he asked to be remembered to various members of
the office. Unfortunately, we haven't the space
to print the entire letter, but here are some of
the high points. Sam won't mind our Philadelphia
summers when he comes back, for the temperature in
Iran hits 126 degrees in the shade. Quote--Even
the camels are taking salt tablets--unquote. When
the President visited Iran last December to review
the troops on the post, Sam was 10 feet away in a
front rank as he passed by in a jeep. Sam was also
heckled by Joe E. Brown and saw Frederic March,
Andre Kostelanotz and Lily Pons. Thanks for such
an interesting letter Sam, and don't wait so long
before we hear from you again.

(From G.I. Joe & Jane
column in THE REVIEW...
Third U.S. Civil Service
Region, Sept. 1944,
Vol. 1, No. 3.)

Joseph Evans Brown was an American Actor and comedian. He was one of the most popular American comedians in the 1930's and 1940's. Up through the late 1950's, he was in many successful films.[8]

From the trailer for the film "The Best Years of Our Lives", 1945

Fredric March was a very talented stage and film actor. He is one of only two actors to have won both the Academy Award for film and the Tony Award for theater twice, the other being Helen Hayes.[9]

A cropped photo from 1963.

Andre Kostelanetz was a Russian-born American orchestral conductor and arranger. Andre was best known to modern audiences for a series of easy listening instrumental albums on Columbia Records from the 1940's until 1980.[10]

Lily Pons was a French-American operatic soprano and actress whose active career went from the late 1920's through the early 1970's. Pons was a principal soprano at the Metropolitan Opera in New York City.[11]

In 1944, during World War II, Pons canceled her fall and winter season in New York and instead toured with the USO, entertaining troops with her singing. Her husband Andre Kostelanetz directed a band composed of American soldiers as an accompaniment to her voice. The pair performed at military bases in North Africa, Italy, the Middle East, the Persian Gulf, India and Burma in 1944.[12]

The war was coming closer to an end, and Sam's civilian life was about to start up again. He went on to create a few more articles for Army publications before the conclusion of his service. As I've already mentioned, after his time with the Army overseas, he continued to write, taking a position with The Ledger-Enquirer in Columbus, GA.

Succulent sappy kisses and hugs for Mom, Pop, Gilda and Herman...

Saturday, Oct. 21, 1944. Iran (Persia).

Have definitely decided on what I will do for the post war era...Have decided to give up writing (will always write a bit now and then) and take some mechanical course in a night technical school! Most likely it will be carpentry! And then will pursue in earnest my hobby of gadgeteering and in time with Sam K. hope to develop something out of it into a business of our own!

I have retyped for clarity.

Saturday, Oct. 21, 1944.
Iran (Persia).

Succulent sappy kisses and hugs for Mom, Pop, Gilda, and Herman...

Have definitely decided on what I will do for the post war era... Have decided to give up writing (will always write a bit now and then) and take some mechanical course in a night technical school! Most likely it will be carpentry! And then will pursue in earnest my hobby of gadgeteering and in time with Sam K. hope to develop something out of it into a business of our own!

Sam took many photos of civilians in Iran. Here are a couple of shots.

NATIVES - IRAN - 1944

NATIVES - IRAN - 1944

Smily hugs and   Tuesday, Nov. 7, 1944
kisses for Mom, Pop,   Iran (Persia).
Gilda and Herman...
                    "WAS IT YOU?"
Someone started the whole day wrong,
     Was it you?
Someone robbed the day of its song,
     Was it you?
Early this morning someone frowned,
Someone sulked until others scowled,
And soon harsh words were passed around,
     Was it you?
Someone started the day aright,
     Was it you?
Someone made it happy and bright,
     Was it you?
Early this morning, we are told,
Someone smiled, and all through the day
This encouraged young and old,
     Was it you?
                    --Stewart I. Long.

Here is a reprint of the scan for clarity.

                              Tuesday, Nov. 7, 1944
                                   Iran (Persia)

Smily hugs and kisses for Mom, Pop, Gilda, and
Herman...

                    "WAS IT YOU?"

Someone started the whole day wrong,
     Was it you?
Someone robbed the day of its song,
     Was it you?
Early this morning someone frowned,
Someone sulked until others scowled,
And soon harsh words were passed around,
     Was it you?
Someone started the day aright,
     Was it you?

Someone made it happy and bright,
    Was it you?
Early this morning, we are told,
    Someone smiled, and all through the day
This encouraged young and old,
    Was it you?

                              --Stewart I. Long

Of the next two photos, the first is in Teheran, Iran, in what Sam calls "the native section" with a mosque in the background. It was taken in 1944.

The third photo was taken in 1944 in Basra, Iraq. It appears to be of two brothers.

In December 1944, Sam got a furlough. He visited Bethlehem and
Jerusalem. The following photos were some he took on that furlough
while visiting a number of the many famous sites in this religiously
diverse area.

This photo shows a street in Bethlehem with farmers selling their
produce.

Geographically, Bethlehem is within the borders of Israel;
however Bethlehem is in an area called the West Bank, which
is an autonomous area administered by the Palestinian
Authority. It is 6.2 miles south of Jerusalem. The Hebrew
Bible identifies it as the city where David was from and
where he became crowned as the King of Israel. The New
Testament identifies Bethlehem as the birthplace of Jesus.[13]

It is also the site of The Church of the Nativity, built over a cave said to have been where Jesus was born. New Testament scriptures say that Jesus was born in a stable associated with an inn, but there is nothing written in the Bible to clarify whether the stable was located in a cave or not.

This photo shows Rachel's tomb, located at the northern entrance to Bethlehem. It is one of Judaism's holiest sites.

It is the site revered as the burial place of the matriarch Rachel as mentioned in the Jewish Bible, the Christian Old Testament and in Muslim literature. The tomb has been considered holy to Jews and Christians for 2,000 years, and to Muslims for 1,400 years. Although this site is deemed to be unlikely to be the actual site of the grave, it is by far the most recognized candidate. Throughout history, the place was rarely considered a shrine exclusive to one religion and is held in esteem equally by Jews, Muslims, and Christians.[14]

The Shepherd's Fields–Bethlehem In Distance

Located approximately 2 km to the east of Bethlehem is the village of Beit Sahour, home of the fields where the Angel of the Lord visited the shepherds and informed them of Jesus' birth, according to Luke 2: 8–10 of the New Testament.[15]

Here is a view of Bethlehem from the south.

Jewelers in Bethlehem working with mother of pearl.

The Church of the Nativity is the oldest church still in use in the Holy Land. The original church was built beginning in 326 AD by Emperor Constantine and his mother Saint Helena. They built the church over the cave, the Grotto of the Nativity, where local history asserts Jesus Christ was born. The present church was built during the reign of the Byzantine Emperor, Justinian in 529 AD.[16]

The following photo shows Church of the Nativity Christmas Services in 1944. The incoming light made an uplifting spiritual service.

Here are a couple of photos of Church of the Nativity Christmas bells. In the second photo, Sam misspelled belfry.

The Church of the Nativity's focal point, The Grotto, is entered via a flight of steps by the church altar.

> The Grotto of the Nativity, the place where Jesus is said to have been born, is an underground space which forms the crypt of the Church of the Nativity. This spot where Jesus was born is marked beneath this altar by a 14-pointed silver star.[17]

You can see that star at the center of the bottom of the photo.

Photo of the church interior, the Nave. The Nave is a central part of a church building intended to accommodate the congregation.

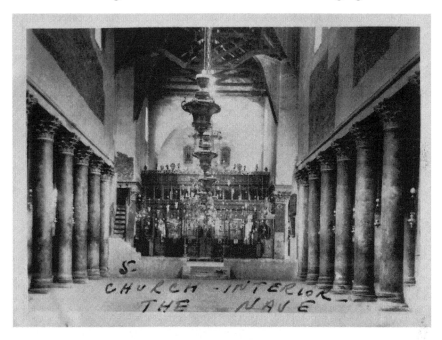

We see 44 columns separating the aisles from each other and from the nave, some of which we find painted with images of saints, such as the Irish monk St. Cathal, the patron of the Sicilian Normans, St. Canute, king of Denmark, and St. Olaf, king of Norway.[18]

The Manger, situated on the north side of the Grotto of the Nativity.[19]

Sam simply titled this photograph "The Tomb."

It is possibly the tomb of Saint Eusebius of Cremona who was head of the monastery. The tombs of Saints Paula and Eustochium are in a room on the left and there is also a tomb for Saint Jerome, whose remains are now in Rome.[20]

Sam visited the Old City of Jerusalem.

> The Old City is a 0.9 square kilometers walled area within the
> modern city of Jerusalem. The Old City is roughly divided
> (going counterclockwise from the northeastern corner) into
> the Muslim Quarter, Christian Quarter, Armenian Quarter
> and Jewish Quarter. The Old City's high defensive walls and
> city gates built in the years 1535–1542 by the Turkish sultan
> Suleiman the Magnificent.[21]

This is a map of the Old City of Jerusalem showing the four quarters
and the Temple Mount areas with the locations of the city gates. (See
number 1 on the Old City of Jerusalem map.)

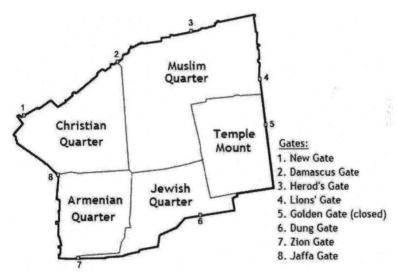

File: OldCityMap.png[22]

The New Gate is the newest gate in the walls that surround
the Old City of Jerusalem It was built in 1889 to provide
direct access between the Christian Quarter and the new
neighborhoods then going up outside the walls.[23]

The Ottoman Sultan Abdul Hamid II allowed the building of the
New Gate.[24]

(Number 2 on the Old City of Jerusalem map.)

The following two photos are of the Damascus Gate.

In this photo, Sam called it St–Stephen's Gate. (St. Stephen's Gate/
The Lion's Gate/Sheep Gate is #4 on the map.)

Lion's Gate also St. Stephen's Gate or Sheep Gate is an
open gate located on the Eastern Wall of the Old City in
Jerusalem.[27]

Carved into the wall above the gate are four lions, two on
the left and two on the right. Suleiman the Magnificent had
the carving made to celebrate the Ottoman defeat of the
Mamluks in 1517. Suleiman the Magnificent built Lion's
Gate in 1542.[28]

The photo here is the
Golden Gate. (Number 5
on the map.)

The Hebrew name
of the Golden Gate
is Gate of Mercy. In
Jewish sources, the
eastern gate of the
Temple compound
is called the Shushan
Gate. If the Golden
Gate does preserve
the location of the
Shushan Gate, which
is only a presumption
with no archaeologi-
cal proof, this will make it the oldest of the current gates in
Jerusalem's Old City Walls.[29]

First walled up in 810, reopened in 1102 by the Crusaders,
then ordered to be walled up by Saladin after regaining Jerusalem in 1187. When Ottoman Sultan Suleiman the Magnificent rebuilt it together with the city walls, but walled it up
in 1541, and it stayed that way.

In Jewish tradition the Golden Gate is the gate through which
the Messiah will enter Jerusalem. Suleiman the Magnificent sealed off the Golden Gate to prevent a false Messiah
or "Anti-christ" coming through entrance. The Ottomans
also built a cemetery in front of the gate, to prevent a false
precursor to the Anointed One, Elijah from passing through
the gate.[30]

Sam's photo was taken before the gate was widened. (The Dung Gate is number 6 on the map.)

The Dung Gate, built in the 16th century, is the gate situated near the southeast corner of the Old City, southwest of the Temple Mount. The 16th-century gate was much smaller but was enlarged in 1952 after the Old City came under Jordanian control in 1948. After its capture by Israel in 1967, renovation occurred.[31]

This gate is probably named after the residue that was taken from the Jewish Temple into the Valley of Hinnon, where it was burned.[32]

The photo after Israeli renovation.

These two photos are of Zion Gate. Sam took the first photo in December 1944, where the second photo was created on July 25, 2006, by Djstatic33-commonwiki. (The Zion Gate is number 7 on the map.)

In the second photo, you can see the effects of the 1967 Arab-Israeli war.

Zion Gate, built in July 1540, was a direct continuation of the Street of the Jews. In the second half of the nineteenth century, a leper colony, and livestock market found in the vicinity of Zion Gate. Towards the end of the nineteenth century, shops located along the length of the southern wall were torn down during the British Mandate.[33]

During the subsequent 1948 Arab-Israeli War, a large number of Jerusalem's churches, convents, mosques, synagogues, monasteries, and cemeteries were put under gunfire or hit by shell. During the Battle for Jerusalem, fighting in the Jewish quarter between the Jordanian Arab Legion and the IDF, Irgun and Lehi had been particularly fierce, leaving the zone in ruins. After the surrender to the Jordanian Arab Legion, the Red Cross, which had been invested with the authority to protect many major sites oversaw the evacuation westwards through Zion Gate of some 1,300 Jews from the Old Quarter.[34]

The following is a photo that Sam took of Jaffa Gate. (Jaffa Gate is number 8 on the map.)

Jaffa Gate was built in 1538 by the Ottoman Empire. Next to the gate is a breach in the wall. It was created in 1898 to allow German emperor Wilhelm II to enter the city triumphally. The breach and the ramp leading up to it allow cars to access the Old City from the west.

The Jaffa Gate has the shape of a medieval gate tower with an L-shaped entryway, secured at both ends (north and east) with heavy doors. The L shape of the old gateway was a classical defensive measure designed to slow down oncoming attackers.[35]

Still on furlough and inside the Old City walls, Sam took the following
photo and titled it "Jew's Wailing Wall."

The Western Wall, Wailing Wall, is an ancient limestone wall in the Old City of Jerusalem. It is a relatively small segment of a far longer ancient retaining wall. The Wall originally was erected as part of the expansion of the Second Jewish Temple begun by Herod the Great. To Jews and Christians, the encased area was known as the Temple Mount.

The Western Wall is considered holy due to its connection to the Temple Mount. Because of the Temple Mount entry restrictions, the Wall is the most sacred place where Jews are permitted to pray. Because of the Jews weeping at the site over the destruction of the Temples, Christians because of this called the Western Wall the Wailing Wall. The term "Wailing Wall" is not used by Jews, and increasingly not by many others who consider it derogatory.[36]

Jewish Prayer on Temple Mount is completely forbidden. Jews may enter only to visit the place, and only at limited times. Muslims are free to pray on Temple Mount, however, Christians and Jews may only visit the site as tourists. They are forbidden from singing, praying, or making any kind of "religious displays".[37]

When researching the Western Wall, I came upon a website called Jewish Virtual Library that is an American-Israeli cooperative enterprise (AICE). They have a photograph section which includes pictures of the Western Wall and there I found Sam's photo of the Western Wall on the top left. I gave them permission to use the photo if they would give credit to Sam Greenberg and correct the photo date. They did so at the bottom of the page under Sources. The URL for the page on the AICE site is: http://www.jewishvirtuallibrary.org/jsource/History/wallpics.html

Sam titled this photo "Jerusalem–and–Mountain–of–Olives." Actually called Mount of Olives, it is located east of the Old City of Jerusalem. There are numerous references to the Mount of Olives in the Old and New Testaments. In the Old Testament, it mentions the Mount of Olives as an escape route for King David during the rebellion of his son, Absalom, then later in the Prophets. In the New Testament, it is noted as being a favorite location for Jesus when teaching his pupils.

Garden of Gethsemane

The Garden of Gethsemane can be found near the foot of
the Mount of Olives. It is named in the New Testament as
the place where Jesus went with his disciples to pray.[38]

The arrest of Jesus was a pivotal event in Christianity
recorded in the canonical gospels. Jesus, a preacher whom
Christians believe to be the Son of God, was arrested by the
Temple guards in the Garden of Gethsemane. The event
ultimately led to Jesus' crucifixion.[39]

Here we see a Judean Home.

This is a photo of Via Dolorosa, a street in the Muslim quarter of the Old City of Jerusalem.

The Via Dolorosa is believed to be the path that Jesus walked on the way to his crucifixion. There have been different routes projected, but the current route has been established since the 18th century. There are 14 Stations of the Cross, nine along the way with the last five stations being inside the Church of the Holy Sepulchre.[40]

The Arch of Ecce Homo.

> Hadrian built a triple-arched
> gateway. The gate was alleged
> to be the location of Jesus' trial.[41]

The Church of the Holy Sepulchre

The site includes both the sites of the crucifixion and the tomb of Jesus of Nazareth.[42]

Sam titled the following photo: "The Citadel"

The Tower of David, also known as the Jerusalem Citadel, is an ancient citadel located near the Jaffa Gate entrance to the western edge of the Old City of Jerusalem.[43]

The title of Sam's next photo is: "Dome–of the–Rock Moriah."

This structure, located on Mount Moriah, is known as the Temple Mount in the Old City of Jerusalem. It was completed in 691 and is one of the oldest works of Islamic architecture.[44]

The Foundation Stone is the name of the rock at the center of the Dome of the Rock in Jerusalem. It is also known as the Pierced Stone because it has a small hole on the southeastern corner that enters a cavern beneath the rock, known as the Well of Souls. According to those that hold it was the site of the Holy of Holies, that would make this the

holiest site in Judaism. Jewish tradition views the Holy of
Holies as the spiritual junction of Heaven and Earth.[45]

The photo is titled: "Temple Area". The Dome of the Rock is visible in
the center. The domed building further back is the Al-Aqsa Mosque.

The following are Sam's photos. They show some of the life activities
in a Kibbutz. They are untitled but self-explanatory. The first photo
is of a beekeeper maintaining hives of honey bee colonies.

The beekeeper, or apiarist, keeps bees in order to collect their honey and other products that the hive produces. These include beeswax, propolis, flower pollen, bee pollen, and royal jelly. Other reasons for keeping bees include pollination of crops and having bees for sale to other beekeepers. The location is called an apiary or bee yard.[46]

A kibbutz is a collective community in Israel that formed traditionally on agriculture. The first Kibbutz evolved in 1909. Today, farming as a significant role in the Kibbutz has changed into other economic branches, including industrial plants and high-tech enterprises.

Kibbutzim began as utopian communities, a combination of socialism and Zionism. In recent decades, some kibbutzim have privatized, thus changes made in the communal lifestyle.

In 2010, there were 270 kibbutzim in Israel. Their factories and farms account for 9% of Israel's industrial output, worth US $8 billion, and 40% of its agricultural production, worth over $1.7 billion.[47]

Photo of a chicken coop with the female chickens feeding outside in the yard.

Inside, the chicken coops have nest boxes for laying eggs and perches where the birds sleep.[48]

This photo is of a dairy where cows are milked and dairy products such as butter, cheese or yogurt are processed.

This is a photo of a field being plowed.

Here are a few photos showing some gardening work.

Chapter Seven

1945

Your Darling Daughter, Charlotte, prompted
me to read "The Razor's Edge" by Somerset
Maugham (am almost through) and lines that
click are: "Because American women expect to
find in their husbands a perfection that Eng-
lish women only hope to find in their butlers."
(re strumpets, harlots or what have you):
"That doesn't mean she's bad. Quite a number
of highly respected citizens get drunk and
have a liking for rough trade. They're bad
habits, like biting one's nails, but I don't
know that they're worse than that. I call a
person bad who lies and cheats and is unkind!"

Thass all...Keep well always!

Your Yank in Iran,

Sam.

I'M UNCLEAR AS TO WHOM this letter was written, but that person had
a daughter named Charlotte. In the letter, Sam says that Charlotte
prompted him to read "The Razor's Edge" by Somerset Maugham.
Sam says that he is almost through reading it and there were two lines
he found of particular interest. The first quote is from Part 4, the 6th
chapter. The second quote is in the 4th chapter of Part 5.

First published in 1944, The Razor's Edge tells the story of
Larry Darrell, an American pilot traumatized by his experiences in World War I, who sets off in search of some tran-
scendent meaning in his life.

His rejection of conventional life and search for meaningful experience allow him to thrive while the more materialistic characters suffer reversals of fortune.[1]

In this letter to home, written on January 22, 1945, Sam writes about an article he read in True Detective magazine. It was titled: "Isn't That Just Like a Man, By a Woman." He points out this line in particular: "He putters in a workshop over some invention that will revolutionize society but beefs like Kansas City if you ask him to hang a curtain."

Excerpts from True Detective magazine

The following is a copy of that letter.

Monday, Jan. 22, 1945
Iran (Persia)

Love, Hugs, kisses & much affection for Mom, Pop, Gilda & Herman—

Item: Excerpt from article in True Detective Mag: entitled: "Isn't that just like a Man, By a Woman:" "He putters in a workshop over some invention that will revolutionize society but beefs like Kansas City if you ask him to hang a curtain."

January 31, 1945, letter to home.

In an effort to help clarify Sam's handwriting, I'll retype it:

> Commando's Kelly's mother has a wonderful simple
> philosophy: all she asked of her children was that they
> hang up their clothes and not lie or steal! She told us
> many times, "If you want anything and you've got to
> have it, just ask for it. We'll get it for you somehow. Don't
> take something that doesn't belong to you and then lie
> about it. God doesn't like that."

Coming up are some very short poems. They all were published in
February 1945.

This poem is a quatrain using the AABB rhyme scheme

Bus Rider's Lament!
Face the driver—Raise your hand!
Pray that he will understand!
Can't he see me? Is he blind?
Once again I'm left behind!
—Corporal Sam Greenberg

February, 1945

Even though this next poem is printed in five lines, I think it's more of a quatrain with the first line split in two. Whether on purpose or not, I'll never know.

? ? ? ? ? ?
Love's exciting,
Love is strange
The average layman hears.
Man will live it thru the eyes
And women thru the ears!
—Corporal Sam Greenberg

February, 1945

This short poem falls into the two line category called a couplet.

Bachelor's Ode!
I think that I shall never see
A dame that's good enough for me!
—Corporal Sam Greenberg

February, 1945

This last poem is a quatrain.

? ? ? ? ? ? ? ?
Pity the goldfish
Who never goes aground;
Travels in the best of circles
Yet never gets "around!"
—Corporal Sam Greenberg.

Sam sent his last V-mail on January 22, 1945, to his mother, Anna
Greenberg, for Valentine's Day in February.

The following group of scans and photos are from Iraq at the beginning of February 1945. This first scan is a menu from the River Front Hotel, Baghdad, Iraq, February 13, 1945

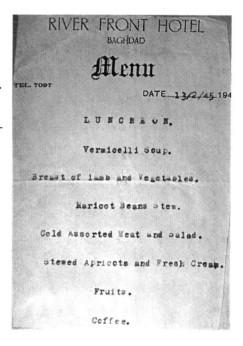

The Faisal Bridge into Baghdad, Iraq, February 1945.

We can see Main Street, Baghdad. The Metro Goldwyn Mayer movie
theater can be seen on the right.

Here is another view of Main Street, Baghdad at night after a rain
storm.

A group of young Iraqis.

The Cast lion in Basra, located on the eastern side of Iraq.

One of Sam's last army publications, published in March 1945. In this article, Sam wrote the first quatrain.

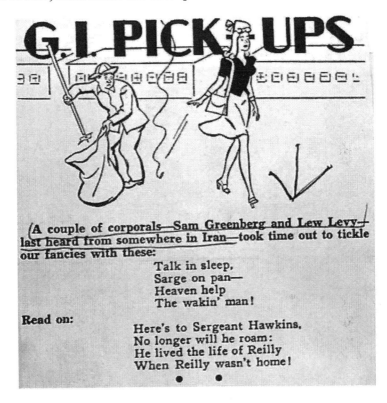

A couple of corporals—Sam Greenberg and Lew Levy—last heard from somewhere in Iran—took time out to tickle our fancies with these:

> Talk in sleep,
> Sarge on pan—
> Heaven help
> The wakin' man!

Read on:

> Here's to Sergeant Hawkins,
> No longer will he roam:
> He lived the life of Reilly
> When Reilly wasn't home!

This is Sam's last war correspondent publication, published in March 1945.

Broken Marriage!
Little digs
Are the things
That gives
A broken marriage
WINGS!
—Corporal Sam Greenberg
MARCH 1945

Chapter Eight

AFTER THE WAR

AFTER THE WAR, Sam Greenberg continued to pursue his interest in writing for the public. He had worked in the newspaper industry since graduating from high school where he first began to hone his writing skills and learn about the newspaper industry, but he wanted to live in a small town and leave behind metropolises like Miami and Philadelphia. He had also spent time in Atlanta, Georgia during the early part of his military career and Atlanta, too, was a little too large. He was drawn to life in Columbus, Georgia, so he and his wife, Ruth, moved there and he went to work for the morning Columbus Enquirer and the afternoon Columbus Ledger.

> The Columbus Enquirer was founded in 1874 and became the morning edition. The afternoon paper was the Columbus Ledger founded in 1886. It became the afternoon edition. In 1988 the two publications merged adopting the name Columbus Ledger-Enquirer.[1]

This is a photo of Sam in Columbus, Georgia on 05/25/1946.

The next two photos are of Sam at work at The Columbus Ledger-Enquirer in 1957.

This first photo was taken in 04/1957.

In 05/1957, dad at work in collaboration.

The following year, 1958, Sam arranged for me to go to the Columbus School of Art for artistic instruction. I was seven years old and in the third grade. There, I produced pastel pencil drawings and linoleum block prints. I had a drawing pad that never left my side and I filled every page. Nine of those drawings are included on my website: http://www.surrealprimitive.com.

Sam Greenberg was a wonderful father. He supported the creative skills I had at an early age. I miss him and want to thank him for all of his support, right from the very beginning.

Thank you, dad. Your support was open-ended. You let me freely explore my creativity and never judged what I chose to create. Because of your support, my creative skills were allowed to develop, free from distractions, so I could grow unfettered and become the artistic person I am today.

Chapter Nine

HISTORY

THE PERSIAN GULF SERVICE COMMAND was activated at Camp Lee, Virginia on October 9, 1942. The United States Army developed the M. T. S. or Motor Transport Service which was under the PGCS, Persian Gulf Service Command. Later they were known as the PGC, Persian Gulf Command. My father was stationed at the headquarters of the Persian Gulf Command Service in a newly formed base called Camp Amirabad.

The following is from the excellent web site "PERSIAN GULF COMMAND VETERANS ORGANIZATION World War II" (http://pgcvowwii.homestead.com/home.html) created by the late Robert C. Patterson and his daughter, Druanne Burns Patterson. Ms. Burns Patterson has given us gracious permission to use the following from their website.

> Robert Patterson was with the US Army 516th QuarterMaster Truck Company, Company C 3923rd QuarterMaster Truck Company. Prior to enlisting, he was a civilian truck driver. He entered active service Dec. 15, 1942 and was discharged Dec. 12, 1945. He was a Heavy Truck Driver and drove a 10 ton diesel Mack-Lanova, hauling supplies to the Russian Army, and First and Third Armies. He made minor

repairs while on the road and supervised civilian mechanics in repairs of trucks. Robert Patterson served as a corporal in the Persian Gulf Command.

Starting in 1942, the United States sent thousands of troops to Iran and Iraq specifically to transport war Materiel to Russia. Iran was already occupied by British and Russian troops who were guarding the oil fields and keeping more than a watchful eye on the pro-German Iranians (Persians). Hitler thought it was only a matter of time before his troops, led from the north by General von Paulus and from the west by General Rommel, would decimate the British, the Russians, and the newly-arrived Americans to take possession of the oil fields and the railroad that snaked through the mountains from the Persian Gulf to the Russian border. But von Paulus found that the Russians fought relentlessly for their homeland and endured unspeakable hardships during the siege of Stalingrad until aid from America enabled them to rally. Rommel found that he had his hands full in Africa.

Conditions in Persia were nothing the American troops could have trained for. Those who arrived in the summer of 1942 were welcomed by pouring rain and mud more than a foot deep. This is where they had to pitch their tents to sleep on the ground for the next six months until huts were built. The rainy season was followed by temperatures that rose as high as 170 degrees in the desert sun, accompanied by sand storms that persisted for as long as a week as they constantly changed the landscape. Beyond the vast expanse of desert dunes were the Zagros Mountains with peaks that rose more than 16,000 feet. Temperatures there dropped to 25 degrees below zero with year round snow cover on the mountaintops.

The culture was even more exotic than the terrain. Camel caravans wound their way through the dunes just as they had thousands of years before Alexander the Great. As the seasons changed, the desert nomads drove millions of sheep across the highway for days at a time as they moved their herds to new grazing grounds. But the tribes of nomads were not the benign shepherds they might seem to be. They were fierce warriors bribed by the Germans to attack the Allies' convoys and trains. Actually, the tribes needed no encouragement to raid the supplies going to Russia. Stealing arms and ammunition was their way of life.

Between 1942 and 1945, the United States armed Russia with 192 thousand trucks and thousands of aircraft, combat vehicles, tanks, weapons, ammunition, and petroleum products later estimated as sufficient to maintain 60 combat divisions in the line. Before the construction of the aircraft assembly plant at Abadan, Iran, the American Air Force flew A-20 medium bombers across the Atlantic to Abadan, where they were turned over to Russian flyers who painted the white star, red, and took off for Stalingrad and other sites on the Eastern Front. Army engineers transformed the camel paths into a highway for trucks and improved the railroad with its more than 200 tunnels so trains could carry tanks and tons of other heavy equipment over the mountains. Historians have stated that without the Russian thrust on the Eastern Front, General Eisenhower would have had to delay the invasion of Normandy until 1945 or later, with a great many more casualties than were suffered in the D-Day 1944 invasion.

The Teheran Conference in the fall of 1943, was the meeting of United States President Franklin D. Roosevelt, British

Prime Minister Winston Churchill, and Soviet Premier Joseph Stalin in the capital city of Iran where Allied troops all over the country were on the alert to protect the Big Three. When Hitler's agents made him aware of the location of the conference, he made plans to assassinate the three leaders of the Allies. German paratroopers, some in Russian uniforms, were dropped in several locations, including the outskirts of Teheran, Kasvin and Qom. The assassination of the Big Three and the destruction of some of the railroad tunnels near Qom were their goals, but they were apprehended almost as soon as they touched ground. The Persian Gulf Command, along with British and Russian troops also rounded the Nazi accomplices, and the Big Three completed their conference without incident.

The veterans of the Persian Gulf Command share many experiences little known to anyone else. Their Persian Gulf Veterans Organization has been meeting since 1946, held together for more than half a century by military service to their country in a strange, exotic land.[1]

Chapter Ten

MY DAD'S BOOK OF IDEAS

THE FOLLOWING IMAGES are from a small notebook that Sam started in June of 1943 in Tehran, Iran. This book contains ideas Sam had, hoping to create a business with his partner who was a machinist. In the notebook Sam talks of his machinist partner as "K". On one page Sam makes reference to a Sam Kleger, so I think this was his partner. The last date of entry for invention ideas is 01/03/1945. He made quite an effort to create new and improved products. Fair warning: Sam's descriptions of his ideas were not always grammatically correct and his writing was sometimes difficult to read.

In the beginning of the little notebook, Sam plans to check with the U.S. Patent Office, then turning it over to the National Inventor's Council in Washington, D. C.

The National Inventors Council (NIC) was a United States government organization established in 1940. It was designed to serve as a clearinghouse for inventions with possible military and national defense uses, and to bring these to the attention of the U.S. armed forces.[1]

He told K, who had a basement workshop, about an inventor that used his father's basement workshop to create the machine that made capsules and filled and sealed them. Sam describes a working procedure on page 131.

Here is a scan of that first page.

This page he mostly prints by hand with some cursive. Here are the page and text copies:

Page 131–Working Procedure!

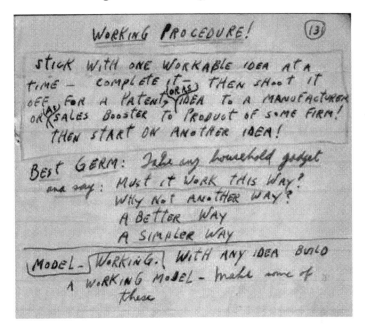

"Stick with one workable idea at a time — complete it — then shoot it off for a patent, or as idea to a manufacturer or as sales booster to product of some firm! Then start on another idea! Best Germ: Take any household gadget and say: Must it work this way? Why not another way? A better way A simpler way. Model–Working. with any idea build a working model–make some of these…"

Page 27–Fishing Gadgets.

"When you go with K's father-in-law keep your eyes open. (there are millions of fishing enthusiasts!) Bait Container attaches to trouser belt. Jar size–has cover attachment that opens with press of finger! One closes upon release of pressure! Spring press tweezer fits into jar for handy use. Cover on jar forces down tweezer (via spring) and it fits into jar. Tweezer has to be long to be able to grasp worm way at bottom of container."

Page 35–Perfume–Jewelry.

"Sell your wares in a solid form (concentrated ?). Tie-up- with jewelry manufacturer sell your lockets, earrings, bracelets (contain perfume packet) (tiny air holes permit scent to waft to escape) Breathing Locket for Perfume! Turn screw & outlet opens & perfume scent escapes or is wafted out! Idea: screw presses against inside of compartment, keeping it closed! Screw loosened & compartment goes back, allowing scent to escape! Compartment narrower at one and widens out to two!"

Page 89–Spring Board–Clip on Pencil.

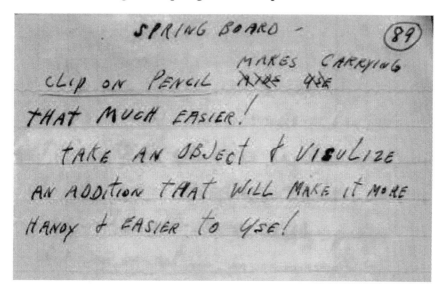

"Clip on Pencil makes carrying that much easier! Take an object and visualize an addition that will make it more handy & easier to use!"

Sam's last entry in the notebook was January 3, 1945.

About the Author

ONE OF THE THINGS for which I will be eternally grateful is that my father recognized very early that I had an artistic inclination and he encouraged it; I started drawing around age three. By the time I was five, Dad brought home a large newsprint drawing pad and a box of charcoal sticks. Some of my earliest drawings were of steel bridges with stick figures on each side of the bridge. I'd draw a battle scene and I gave my stick figures rifles with their bullets shown in stages through time going over to the other side. Dynamite being thrown got the same treatment, leading to a final explosion as it landed. My father always supported me. He never judged or told me what to draw, he just let me produce what I wanted. He never held me back. He let me create and grow.

I had my father until I was 12. He suffered from what was called manic depression in his day, now more commonly referred to as bipolar disorder, and left us by committing suicide. I never really got to know the man he was as I had only a child's perspective, but as I grew older I learned much more about him.

I believe I took after my dad quite a bit, especially in the creative vein. Sam had a passion for writing and literature, where my own is in visually expressing life, as I experience it. The creativity we shared also held another area of kinship: inventions. Perhaps he was always so inclined, but toward the end of his military service, Sam partnered with a machinist who helped build prototypes of his ideas for production. The first idea I had, that I can remember, came when I was around 10 years old and was for a toy. The most recent is a card deck and game I created and produced called "RAFFUS ©1992."

Our household was Conservative Jewish. We never kept kosher in our diet, although I did have a traditional bar mitzvah at the age of thirteen. Being that I lost my dad when I was twelve, talking with him about his religious beliefs just wasn't something that occurred to me to do, so I really don't know where he stood. After my teen years, I became a non-practicing Jew. I believed in God but I did not want to adhere to any organized religion. In my later 30's, I became a spiritual practitioner of what some call the New Age Movement.

I attended Georgia State University where I received an undergraduate degree in 1975, a BVA, Bachelor of Visual Arts. My major was sculpture with a minor in printmaking.

I have a website, https://surrealprimitive.com which is primarily a display of my fine art — sculpture, art prints and posters. The site is a collection of my work, both current and available for purchase, as well as previous projects which have since been sold. "RAFFUS" is also available there. I plan to produce a computer app for this game. For the sake of whimsy, there are also examples of my earliest artwork shown, from 1958 at age seven.

I have another website, https://www.redbubble.com/people/dwardlee/shop, Redbubble is a global marketplace for independent artists. I have the following products available, and many more, T-shirts, vinyl stickers, device cases, posters, etc.

"Like Father, Like Son"

MANY WOULD ASSUME because I am involved with The New Age Movement that I would hold liberal/progressive views, but they would be mistaken.

My father and I believed in most of the tenants of conservatism. My father found a way to turn his literary passions into a pastime in the U.S. Army as a war correspondent. I work as a metal fabricator, a job closely related to my creative direction; you can see examples of my metal sculpture on my website. We both knew that we had almost limitless opportunities as citizens of the United States and found our niches in workplaces that reflected our creative sides. Those "side jobs"—when my dream would be to live as an artist—have afforded me excellent and varied experiences that have enriched my life.

How many people can say that they spent almost a year on top of their state capitol building, stripping away the old gold leaf? We were preparing the dome for a new gold leaf. All these things contribute toward expanding a facet of my artistic expression.

On other conservative points, take, for example, the politically charged topic of illegal immigration. It's hard for me to understand how I could be demeaned and considered racist when I have lived in other countries with the full intention of marrying someone from that area. My conservative values dictate, though, that actions in life should be done lawfully and according to the established order. Don't like the order? Change it, not by breaking the law, but by adequately petitioning to change the code. I am against illegal immigration. Every unauthorized immigrant not only violates our rules to be here but then takes advantage of the generous programs in our country that are to help those in need. My father, when exposed to the Persian culture, saw great value in a society that valued the contributions and wisdom of women. At much earlier times, there were great female leaders in Iran and helped to make their country great. Neither of us was closed off to appreciating what another culture can contribute, just because it was different from what we knew by our birth.

I could go through many other issues, point by point, but let it just be said that in many ways, my father and I were very much alike. I am proud of my dad's accomplishments and I wish he had lived long enough to see what I have done with the talents he fostered in me at such a young age. I feel certain he would be proud of me, as well.

I am so thankful that my dad was one to keep records. It was through his scrapbook and photo albums that I really got to know him.

———

As for me, I was born in Columbus, Georgia in 1950 as Edward Mark Greenberg. I changed my name in 1986 to Dward Lee Greenbird. I live in Stone Mountain, Georgia.

Prayers for Our World

I PRAY FOR RELIGIOUS and spiritual harmony between all factions of religious and spiritual believers. I invoke that all individuals be happy and content if they believe that they have the spiritual answer to our reality. I ask that those individuals not feel compelled to change the mind of another person who has a different belief. I ask for open-mindedness between all groups on our planet, including the atheist and agnostic. We need not concern ourselves if another person has a different perspective than our own religious, spiritual reality. There are infinitely many other positive ideas that one can pursue as a life's mission or purpose. One should want to help humanity by making the world a better place for all of us to live and to work toward becoming who we are.

I pray for Love as healing, forgiveness, compassion, clarity, equality, justice, and wisdom to heal all people. I pray to God for humanity to manifest stability, higher consciousness, being, and harmony for themselves, individually, and between themselves in their relationships with others. For understanding, I pray for universal peace, cosmic Love, cosmic integrity, infinite clarity, and cosmic forgiveness.

I pray for humanity that God removes negative records, patterns, and illusions from all peoples. These negatives pertain to but are not limited to Intolerance, family/clan beliefs, karma, and fear resulting in hatred and distrust of those who are different and have different ideas. I invoke to replace those negative records, patterns, and illusions with, but not limited to: global consciousness, tolerance, compassion, Love, self-responsibility, and an improved spiritual connection to God and all of nature.

I pray that all humans recognize that we are one, that life is sacred, that diversity is a creative force. May all beings experience oneness with God as they understand God to be. Love is the most potent energy in the Universe. I resolve to be a conduit and channel love out into the world for this healing.

The following is a list some quotes from famous spiritual teachers regarding different religions on our planet and how all religious paths will lead the individual to God.

Mahatma Gandhi:

Mahatma Gandhi was from India was an advocate and pioneer of nonviolent social protest and direct action in the form he called Satyagraha. He led the struggle for India's independence from British colonial rule.[1]

For me, the different religions are beautiful flowers from the same garden, or they are branches of the same majestic tree. Therefore they are equally authentic, though being received and interpreted through human instruments equally imperfect.[2]

Ramakrishna:

Ramakrishna was an Indian mystic.[3]

One should not think, "My religion alone is the right path, and other religions are false." God becomes more conscious by utilizing all paths. It is enough to have sincere yearning for God. Infinite are the paths and countless opinions.[4]

Thich Nhat Hanh:

> Thich Nhat Hanh is an expatriate Vietnamese Buddhist monk, peace activist, and author.[5]

> Here Love is the capacity to take care, to protect, to nourish. If you are not capable of generating that kind of energy toward yourself — if you are not capable of taking care of yourself, of feeding yourself, of protecting yourself — it is challenging to take care of another person.

> To rally people, governments need enemies. They want us to be afraid, to hate so that we will rally behind them. So if they do not have a real enemy, they will invent one to mobilize us.[6]

Zoroaster:

> Zoroaster was the prophet of the Zoroastrian religion. There is an opinion that he lived in eastern Iran or central Asia around 1000 BC. The Gathas are hymns held by believers to have been written by Zoroaster.[7]

I found the following lines in Zoroaster's Gathas or hymns.

> He who upholds Truth with all the might of his power,
>
> He who upholds Truth the utmost in his word and deed,
>
> He, indeed, is Thy most valued helper, O Mazda Ahura!
>
> He who abhors and shuns the light of the Sun,
>
> He who refuses to behold with respect the living creation of God,
>
> He who leads the good to wickedness,

He who makes the meadows waterless and the pastures desolate,

He who lets fly his weapon against the innocent,

An enemy of my faith, a destroyer of Thy principles is he, O Lord!

A righteous government is of all the most to be wished for,

Bearing of blessing and good fortune in the highest.

Guided by the law of Truth, supported by dedication and zeal,

It blossoms into the Best of Order, a Kingdom of Heaven!

To effect this I shall work now and ever more.[8]

Endnotes

A Note on Endnotes

In some cases, I changed the wording of some endnotes to fit the style of the book. All sources given are accurate as of the date of the research.

———

Chapter One: My Fathers's Albums and Scrapbook:

[1] Wikipedia contributors. "U. S. Army airships." Wikipedia, The Free Encyclopedia. Wikipedia, The Free Encyclopedia, 25 November 2019. Web. 13 January 2020. https://en.wikipedia.org/wiki/U.S._Army_airships

Chapter Four: 1942

[1] Contributors to The National Archives at Atlanta. "Office of the Chief of Ordnance, 1940 – 1966; Atlanta Ordnance Depot, p.12, Section: Brief History;" The National Archives at Atlanta. 5780 Jonesboro Road, Morrow, GA 30260. May – July 2013. 4 May 2018. https://www.archives.gov/files/atlanta/finding-aids/rg-156-chief-of-ordnance-facilities.pdf

[2] Eric Carpenter. "File:Judy Garland publicity photo.png." Wikimedia Commons, the free media repository. Wikimedia Foundation, Inc., 149 New Montgomery St., 6th Floor, San Francisco, CA 94105. 16 Jan. 2018. 02 June 2018. https://commons.wikimedia.org/wiki/File:Judy_Garland_publicity_photo.png#

[3] Wikipedia contributors. "Judy Garland." Wikipedia, The Free

Encyclopedia. Wikipedia, The Free Encyclopedia, 1 Sep. 2018. Web. 2 Sep. 2018. https://en.wikipedia.org/wiki/Judy_Garland

[4] Wikipedia contributors. "Judy Garland; Section: The Wizard of Oz." Wikipedia, The Free Encyclopedia. Wikipedia, The Free Encyclopedia, 1 Sep. 2018. Web. 2 Sep. 2018. https://en.wikipedia.org/wiki/Judy_Garland

Chapter Five: 1943

[1] Wikipedia contributors. "Photoplay." Wikipedia, The Free Encyclopedia. Wikipedia, The Free Encyclopedia, 7 Apr. 2018. Web. 8 Apr. 2018. https://en.wikipedia.org/wiki/Photoplay

[2] Wikipedia contributors. "Sasanian Empire" Wikipedia, The Free Encyclopedia. Wikipedia, The Free Encyclopedia, 13 May 2019. Web, 16 May 2019. https://en.wikipedia.org/wiki/Sasanian_Empire

[3] Wikipedia contributors. "Asadabad, Iran" Wikipedia, The Free Encyclopedia. Wikipedia, The Free Encyclopedia, 1 August 2018. Web. 16 May 2018. https://en.wikipedia.org/wiki/Asadabad,_Iran

[4] Wikipedia contributors. "Avicenna" Wikipedia, The Free Encyclopedia. Wikipedia, The Free Encyclopedia, 13 May 2019. Web. 16 May 2019. https://en.wikipedia.org/wiki/Avicenna

[5] Wikipedia contributors. "James Roosevelt." Wikipedia, The Free Encyclopedia. Wikipedia, The Free Encyclopedia, 23 Sep. 2018. Web. 6 Oct. 2018. https://en.wikipedia.org/wiki/James_Roosevelt

[6] Wikipedia contributors, "Esther." Wikipedia, The Free Encyclopedia. Wikipedia, The Free Encyclopedia, 10 May 2019, Web. 17 May, 2019. https://en.wikipedia.org/wiki/Esther

[7] Wikipedia contributors, "Mordecai–Section: Biblical account" Wikipedia, The Free Encyclopedia. Wikipedia, The Free Encyclopedia,

19 May 2019. 20 May 2019. https://en.wikipedia.org/wiki/Mordecai

[8] Wikipedia contributors. "Darius the Great." Wikipedia, The Free Encyclopedia. Wikipedia, The Free Encyclopedia, 20 May 2019. Web. 20 May 2019. https://en.wikipedia.org/wiki/Darius_the_Great

[9] Wikipedia contributors. "Persian Corridor." Wikipedia, The Free Encyclopedia. Wikipedia, The Free Encyclopedia, 13 March 2019. Web. 21 May 2019. https://en.wikipedia.org/wiki/Persian_Corridor

[10] Wikipedia contributors. "Anglo-Soviet invasion of Iran–Section: Occupation" Wikipedia, The Free Encyclopedia. Wikipedia, The Free Encyclopedia, 11 May 2019. Web. 21 May 2019. https://en.wikipedia.org/wiki/Anglo-Soviet_invasion_of_Iran

[11] Wikipedia contributors. "Old Bridge of Dezful." The Free Encyclopedia. Wikipedia, The Free Encyclopedia, 28 March 2019, Web. 26 August 2019. https://en.wikipedia.org/wiki/Old_Bridge_of_Dezful

[12] Wikipedia contributors. "Shush Castle" Wikipedia, The Free Encyclopedia. Wikipedia, The Free Encyclopedia, 4 March 2019. Web. 22 May 2019. https://en.wikipedia.org/wiki/Shush_Castle

[13] Wikipedia contributors. "Sasanian Empire–Section: Second Golden Era (489 – 622)" Wikipedia, The Free Encyclopedia. Wikipedia, The Free Encyclopedia, 22 May 2019. Web. 22 May 2019. https://en.wikipedia.org/wiki/Sasanian_Empire

[14] Wikipedia contributors. "V-mail." Wikipedia, The Free Encyclopedia. Wikipedia, The Free Encyclopedia, 16 Jan. 2018. Web. 8 Apr. 2018. https://en.wikipedia.org/wiki/V-mail

[15] Wikipedia contributors. "Falak-ol-Aflak Castle". Wikipedia, The Free Encyclopedia. Wikipedia, The Free Encyclopedia, 3 May 2019. Web. 23 May 2019. https://en.wikipedia.org/wiki/Falak-ol-Aflak_Castle

[16] Wikipedia contributors. "Omar Khayyam." Wikipedia, The Free

Encyclopedia. Wikipedia, The Free Encyclopedia, 21 May 2019. Web. 23 May 2019. https://en.wikipedia.org/wiki/Omar_Khayyam

[17] Wikipedia contributors. "Rosh Hashanah." Wikipedia, The Free Encyclopedia. Wikipedia, The Free Encyclopedia, 24 April 2019. Web. 27 May 2019. https://en.wikipedia.org/wiki/Rosh_Hashanah

[18] Wikipedia contributors. "Repentance in Judaism." Wikipedia, The Free Encyclopedia. Wikipedia, The Free Encyclopedia, 23 March 2019. Web. 27 May 2019. https://en.wikipedia.org/wiki/Repentance_in_Judaism

[19] Wikipedia contributors. "Yom Kippur." Wikipedia, The Free Encyclopedia. Wikipedia, The Free Encyclopedia, 19 May 2019. Web. 27 May 2019. https://en.wikipedia.org/wiki/Yom_Kippur

[20] Wikipedia contributors. "Qazvin–section: History." Wikipedia, The Free Encyclopedia. Wikipedia, The Free Encyclopedia, 3 Jan. 2020. 11 Jan. 2020. https://en.wikipedia.org/wiki/Qazvin

[21] Wikipedia contributors. "Susa." Wikipedia, The Free Encyclopedia. Wikipedia, The Free Encyclopedia, 29 May 2019. Web. 29 May 2019. https://en.wikipedia.org/wiki/Susa

[22] Wikipedia contributors. "Jameh Mosque of Qazvin." Wikipedia, The Free Encyclopedia. Wikipedia, The Free Encyclopedia, 29 Apr. 2018. Web. 7 Jul. 2018. https://en.wikipedia.org/wiki/Jameh_Mosque_of_Qazvin

[23] Wikipedia contributors. "Musalla." Wikipedia, The Free Encyclopedia. Wikipedia, The Free Encyclopedia, 10 January 2019 Web. 29 May 2019. https://en.wikipedia.org/wiki/Musalla

[24] Wikipedia contributors. "Citadel." Wikipedia, The Free Encyclopedia. Wikipedia, The Free Encyclopedia, 11 April 2019 Web. 29 May 2019. https://en.wikipedia.org/wiki/Citadel

25 Wikipedia contributors. "Rita Hayworth." Wikipedia, The Free Encyclopedia. Wikipedia, The Free Encyclopedia, 5 Apr. 2018. Web. 8 Apr. 2018. https://en.wikipedia.org/wiki/Rita_Hayworth

26 Ned Scott, Columbia Pictures, photographer. "File:Rita Hayworth-publicity.JPG." Wikimedia Commons, the free media repository. 20 Feb 2018. Web. 27 Jun 2018. https://commons.wikimedia.org/w/index.php?title=File:Rita_Hayworth-publicity.JPG&oldid=288356622

27 Druanne Patterson Burns and Robert Patterson, "History; Section: Who Are You," Persian Gulf Command Veterans Organization World War II, 79 Blue School Road, Danville, PA 17821. Copyright 2009. 8 May 2018. http://pgcvowwii.homestead.com/History.html

Chapter Six: 1944

1 Lindsay "Luna" Blenkarn, "Top Five Lena Horne Films," HubPages; Section: Entertainment and Media, 1111 Broadway, Floor 3 (Room # 169), Oakland, CA 94607. 4 March 2018. 1 August 2018. https://hubpages.com/entertainment/Top-Five-Lena-Horne-Films

2 Wikipedia contributors. "Lena Horne." Wikipedia, The Free Encyclopedia. Wikipedia, The Free Encyclopedia, 27 May 2019. Web. 1 June 2019. https://en.wikipedia.org/wiki/Lena_Horne

3 Wikipedia contributors. "Passover." Wikipedia, The Free Encyclopedia. Wikipedia, The Free Encyclopedia, 4 Apr. 2018. Web. 8 Apr. 2018. https://en.wikipedia.org/wiki/Passover

4 Druanne Burns Patterson and Robert Patterson, "Insignia," Persian Gulf Command Veterans Organization World War II, 79 Blue School Road, Danville, PA 17821, Copyright: 2009. 8 May 2018. http://pgcvowwii.homestead.com/insignia.html

[5] Wikipedia contributors. "Myrna Loy." Wikipedia, The Free Encyclopedia. Wikipedia, The Free Encyclopedia, 20 May 2019. Web. 2 June 2019. https://en.wikipedia.org/wiki/Myrna_Loy

[6] Wikipedia contributors. "Shadow of the Thin Man–Section: Production notes." Wikipedia, The Free Encyclopedia. Wikipedia, The Free Encyclopedia, 8 Jan. 2018. Web. 8 Apr. 2018. https://en.wikipedia.org/wiki/Shadow_of_the_Thin_Man

[7] Wikipedia contributors. "Ken Maynard."–Section: Biography, Wikipedia, The Free Encyclopedia. Wikipedia, The Free Encyclopedia, 20 May 2019. Web. 2 June 2019. https://en.wikipedia.org/wiki/Ken_Maynard

[8] Wikipedia contributors. "Joe E. Brown." Wikipedia, The Free Encyclopedia. Wikipedia, The Free Encyclopedia, 14 Feb. 2018. Web. 8 Apr. 2018. https://en.wikipedia.org/wiki/Joe_E._Brown

[9] Wikipedia contributors. "Fredric March." Wikipedia, The Free Encyclopedia. Wikipedia, The Free Encyclopedia, 31 December 2019. Web. 12 Jan. 2020. https://en.wikipedia.org/wiki/Fredric_March

[10] Wikipedia contributors. "Andre Kostelanetz." Wikipedia, The Free Encyclopedia. Wikipedia, The Free Encyclopedia, 1 Mar. 2018. Web. 8 Apr. 2018. https://en.wikipedia.org/wiki/Andre_Kostelanetz

[11] Wikipedia contributors. "Lily Pons." Wikipedia, The Free Encyclopedia. Wikipedia, The Free Encyclopedia, 23 May 2019. Web. 3 June 2019. https://en.wikipedia.org/wiki/Lily_Pons

[12] Wikipedia contributors. "Lily Pons"–Section: Career, Wikipedia, The Free Encyclopedia. Wikipedia, The Free Encyclopedia, 23 May 2019. Web. 3 June 2019. https://en.wikipedia.org/wiki/Lily_Pons

[13] Wikipedia contributors. "Bethlehem." Wikipedia, The Free Encyclopedia. Wikipedia, The Free Encyclopedia, 7 Apr. 2018. Web. 8

Apr. 2018. https://en.wikipedia.org/wiki/Bethlehem

[14] Wikipedia contributors. "Rachel's Tomb." Wikipedia, The Free Encyclopedia. Wikipedia, The Free Encyclopedia, 27 May 2019. Web. 4 June 2019. https://en.wikipedia.org/wiki/Rachel's_Tomb

[15] Contributors to Palestine Ministry of Tourism and Antiquities; "Shepherds' Field, Bethlehem," Atlas Travel & Tourist Agency, Atlas Travel & Tourist Agency, King Hussein Street, P.O. Box 7131, Amman, 11118, Jordan. 1997 – 2018. 30 July 2018. http://www.atlastours.net/holyland/shepherds_field.html

[16] Contributors to Palestine Ministry of Tourism and Antiquities; "Church of the Nativity, Bethlehem," Atlas Travel & Tourist Agency, Atlas Travel & Tourist Agency, King Hussein Street, P.O. Box 7131, Amman, 11118, Jordan. 1997 – 2018. 21 Septem- ber 2018. http://www.atlastours.net/holyland/church_of_the_nativity.html

[17] Wikipedia contributors. "Church of the Nativity–Section: Grotto of the Nativity." Wikipedia, The Free Encyclopedia. Wikipedia, The Free Encyclopedia, 14 May 2019. Web. 4 June 2019. https://en.wikipedia.org/wiki/Church_of_the_Nativity

[18] Wikipedia contributors. "Church of the Nativity–Section: Church, or Basilica, of the Nativity." Wikipedia, The Free Encyclopedia. Wikipedia, The Free Encyclopedia, 14 May 2019. Web. 4 June 2019. https://en.wikipedia.org/wiki/Church_of_the_Nativity

[19] Contributors to Palestine Ministry of Tourism and Antiquities; "Church of the Nativity, Bethlehem," Atlas Travel & Tourist Agency, Atlas Travel & Tourist Agency, King Hussein Street, P.O. Box 7131, Amman, 11118, Jordan. 1997 – 2018. 30 July 2018. http://www.atlastours.net/holyland/church_of_the_nativity.html

[20] Contributors to Palestine Ministry of Tourism and Antiquities; "Church of the Nativity, Bethlehem," Atlas Travel & Tourist Agency,

Atlas Travel & Tourist Agency, King Hussein Street, P.O. Box 7131, Amman, 11118, Jordan. 1997 – 2018. 30 July 2018. http://www.atlastours.net/holyland/church_of_the_nativity.html

[21] Wikipedia contributors. "Old City (Jerusalem)." Wikipedia, The Free Encyclopedia. Wikipedia, The Free Encyclopedia, 2 June 2019. Web. 5 June 2019. https://en.wikipedia.org/wiki/Old_City_(Jerusalem)

[22] Wikipedia contributors. "File:OldCityMap.PNG." Wikimedia Commons, the free media repository. Wikipedia Commons, The Free Media Repository, 19 Jan 2016. Web. 29 Apr 2018. https://commons.wikimedia.org/w/index.php?title=File:OldCityMap.PNG&oldid=185051914

[23] Wikipedia contributors. "New Gate." Wikipedia, The Free Encyclopedia. Wikipedia, The Free Encyclopedia, 3 April 2019. Web. 6 June 2019. https://en.wikipedia.org/wiki/New_Gate

[24] Wikipedia contributors. "New Gate–Section: Etymology." Wikipedia, The Free Encyclopedia. Wikipedia, The Free Encyclopedia, 3 April 2019. Web. 6 June 2019. https://en.wikipedia.org/wiki/New_Gate

[25] Wikipedia contributors. "Damascus Gate." Wikipedia, The Free Encyclopedia. Wikipedia, The Free Encyclopedia, 27 May 2019. Web. 6 June 2019. https://en.wikipedia.org/wiki/Damascus_Gate

[26] Wikipedia contributors. "Damascus Gate–Section: History." Wikipedia, The Free Encyclopedia. Wikipedia, 27 May 2019. Web. 6 June 2019. https://en.wikipedia.org/wiki/Damascus_Gate

[27] Wikipedia contributors. "Lions' Gate." Wikipedia, The Free Encyclopedia. Wikipedia, The Free Encyclopedia, 9 April 2019. Web. 6 June 2019. https://en.wikipedia.org/wiki/Lions%27_Gate

[28] Wikipedia contributors. "Lions' Gate–Section: History." Wikipedia, The Free Encyclopedia. Wikipedia, The Free Encyclopedia,

9 April 2019. Web. 6 June 2019. https://en.wikipedia.org/wiki/Lions%27_Gate

[29] Wikipedia contributors. "Golden Gate (Jerusalem)." Wikipedia, The Free Encyclopedia. Wikipedia, The Free Encyclopedia, 17 May 2019. Web. 7 June 2019. https://en.wikipedia.org/wiki/Golden_Gate_(Jerusalem)

[30] Wikipedia contributors. "Golden Gate (Jerusalem)–Section: The Sealing of the gate." Wikipedia, The Free Encyclopedia. Wikipedia, The Free Encyclopedia, 17 May 2019. Web. 7 June 2019. https://en.wikipedia.org/wiki/Golden_Gate_(Jerusalem)

[31] Wikipedia contributors. "Dung Gate." Wikipedia, The Free Encyclopedia. Wikipedia, The Free Encyclopedia, 13 May 2019. Web. 7 June 2019. https://en.wikipedia.org/wiki/Dung_Gate

[32] Wikipedia contributors. "Dung Gate–Section: Name." Wikipedia, The Free Encyclopedia. Wikipedia, The Free Encyclopedia, 13 May 2019. Web. 8 June 2019. https://en.wikipedia.org/wiki/Dung_Gate

[33] Wikipedia contributors. "Zion Gate–Section: History." Wikipedia, The Free Encyclopedia. Wikipedia, The Free Encyclopedia, 3 April 2019. Web. 9 June 2019. https://en.wikipedia.org/wiki/Zion_Gate

[34] Wikipedia contributors. "East Jerusalem–Section: History: 1948 Arab–Israeli War and aftermath." Wikipedia, The Free Encyclopedia. Wikipedia, The Free Encyclopedia, 5 June 2019. Web. 9 June 2019. https://en.wikipedia.org/wiki/East_Jerusalem

[35] Wikipedia contributors. "Jaffa Gate." Wikipedia, The Free Encyclopedia. Wikipedia, The Free Encyclopedia, 18 May 2019. Web. 9 June 2019. https://en.wikipedia.org/wiki/Jaffa_Gate

[36] Wikipedia contributors. "Western Wall." Wikipedia, The Free

Encyclopedia. Wikipedia, The Free Encyclopedia, 12 June 2019. Web. 12 June 2019. https://en.wikipedia.org/wiki/Western_Wall

[37] Wikipedia contributors. "Temple Mount entry restrictions–Section: Israeli restriction policy." Wikipedia, The Free Encyclopedia. Wikipedia, The Free Encyclopedia, 23 May 2018. Web. 12 June 2019. https://en.wikipedia.org/wiki/Temple_Mount_entry_restrictions

[38] Pat McCarthy, "Gethsemane," Seetheholyland.net, Wernham Place, Northcote, Auckland 0626, New Zealand 2017. 24 July 2018. http://www.seetheholyland.net/gethsemane/

[39] Wikipedia contributors. "Arrest of Jesus." Wikipedia, The Free Encyclopedia. Wikipedia, The Free Encyclopedia, 12 June 2019. Web. 13 June 2019. https://en.wikipedia.org/wiki/Arrest_of_Jesus

[40] Wikipedia contributors. "Via Dolorosa." Wikipedia, The Free Encyclopedia. Wikipedia, The Free Encyclopedia, 24 Jan. 2018. Web. 8 Apr. 2018. https://en.wikipedia.org/wiki/Via_Dolorosa

[41] Wikipedia contributors. "Aelia Capitolina–Section: Ecce homo arch." Wikipedia, The Free Encyclopedia. Wikipedia, The Free Encyclopedia, 30 April 2019. Web. 13 June 2019. https://en.wikipedia.org/wiki/Aelia_Capitolina

[42] Wikipedia contributors. "Church of the Holy Sepulchre." Wikipedia, The Free Encyclopedia. Wikipedia, The Free Encyclopedia, 11 Jul. 2018. Web. 24 Jul. 2018. https://en.wikipedia.org/wiki/Church_of_the_Holy_Sepulchre

[43] Wikipedia contributors. "Tower of David." Wikipedia, The Free Encyclopedia. Wikipedia, The Free Encyclopedia, 2 April 2019. Web. 13 June 2019. https://en.wikipedia.org/wiki/Tower_of_David

[44] Wikipedia contributors. "Dome of the Rock." Wikipedia, The Free Encyclopedia. Wikipedia, The Free Encyclopedia, 15 Feb. 2018.

Web. 8 Apr. 2018. https://en.wikipedia.org/wiki/Dome_of_the_Rock

45 Wikipedia contributors. "Foundation Stone." Wikipedia, The Free Encyclopedia. Wikipedia, The Free Encyclopedia, 11 March 2019. Web. 13 June 2019. https://en.wikipedia.org/wiki/Foundation_Stone

46 Wikipedia contributors. "Beekeeping." Wikipedia, The Free Encyclopedia. Wikipedia, The Free Encyclopedia, 3 Apr. 2018. Web. 8 Apr. 2018. https://en.wikipedia.org/wiki/Beekeeping

47 Wikipedia contributors. "Kibbutz." Wikipedia, The Free Encyclopedia. Wikipedia, The Free Encyclopedia, 6 January 2019. Web. 15 June 2019. https://en.wikipedia.org/wiki/Kibbutz

48 Wikipedia contributors. "Chicken coop." Wikipedia, The Free Encyclopedia. Wikipedia, The Free Encyclopedia, 7 Apr. 2018. Web. 8 Apr. 2018. https://en.wikipedia.org/wiki/Chicken_coop

Chapter Seven: 1945

1 Wikipedia contributors. "The Razor's Edge." Wikipedia, The Free Encyclopedia. Wikipedia, The Free Encyclopedia, 19 Jun. 2018. Web. 8 Jul. 2018. https://en.wikipedia.org/wiki/The_Razor's_Edge

After the War

1 Wikipedia contributors. "Ledger-Enquirer." Wikipedia, The Free Encyclopedia. Wikipedia, The Free Encyclopedia, 22 Jul. 2018. Web. 3 Aug. 2018. https://en.wikipedia.org/wiki/Ledger-Enquirer

History

1 Druanne Patterson Burns and Robert Patterson, "History; Who Are You;" Persian Gulf Command Veterans Organization World War

II, 79 Blue School Road, Danville, PA 17821, Copyright: 2009. 8 May 2018. http://www.pgcvowwii.com/History.html

My Dad's Book of Ideas

[1] Wikipedia contributors. "National Inventors Council." Wikipedia, The Free Encyclopedia. Wikipedia, The Free Encyclopedia, 5 Sep. 2017. Web. 3 Aug. 2018. https://en.wikipedia.org/wiki/National_Inventors_Council

Prayers for Our World

[1] Wikiquote contributors. "Mahatma Gandhi." Wikiquote, The Free Quote Compendium, Wikiquote, The Free Quote Compendium, 4 July 2019. Web. 6 July 2019. https://en.wikiquote.org/wiki/Mahatma_Gandhi

[2] Wikiquote contributors. "Mahatma Gandhi–Section: Posthumous publications (1950s and later)." Wikiquote, The Free Quote Compendium, Wikiquote, The Free Quote Compendium,, 4 July 2019. Web. 6 July 2019. https://en.wikiquote.org/wiki/Mahatma_Gandhi

[3] Wikiquote contributors. "Ramakrishna." Wikiquote, The Free Quote Compendium, Wikiquote, The Free Quote Compen- dium, 11 May 2019. Web. 6 July 2019. https://en.wikiquote.org/wiki/Ramakrishna

[4] Wikiquote contributors. "Ramakrishna–Section: The Gospel of Sri Ramakrishna (1942)." Wikiquote, The Free Quote Compendium, Wikiquote, The Free Quote Compendium, 11 May 2019. Web. 6 July 2019. https://en.wikiquote.org/wiki/Ramakrishna

[5] Wikiquote contributors. "Thich Nhat Hanh." Wikiquote, The Free Quote Compendium, Wikiquote, The Free Quote Compendium,

11 May 2019. Web. 5 July 2019. 6 July 2019. https://en.wikiquote.org/wiki/Thich_Nhat_Hanh

[6] Wikiquote contributors. "Thich Nhat Hanh–Section: Quotes." Wikiquote, The Free Quote Compendium, Wikiquote, The Free Quote Compendium, 11 May 2019. Web. 5 July 2019. 6 July 2019. https://en.wikiquote.org/wiki/Thich_Nhat_Hanh

[7] Wikiquote contributors. "Zoroaster–Section: Quotes." Wikiquote, The Free Quote Compendium, Wikiquote, The Free Quote Compendium, 5 July 2019. Web. 6 July 2019. https://en.wikiquote.org/wiki/Zoroaster

[8] Wikiquote contributors. "Zoroaster–Section: Quotes: The Gathas." Wikiquote, The Free Quote Compendium, Wikiquote, The Free Quote Compendium, 5 July 2019. Web. 6 July 2019. https://en.wikiquote.org/wiki/Zoroaster